"Restaurant patrons looking for quality dining have Zagat to guide their cuisine needs. For the recruitment industry, the name is Weddle... Peter Weddle that is."
American Staffing Association

What People are Saying about WEDDLE's Newsletters, Guides & Directories

"refreshingly unassuming and hype-free text.... It's all excellent stuff ...."
Porter Anderson
CNN

"WEDDLE's is a very useful tool that recruiters and HR professionals will find helpful."
Fortune Magazine

"... a wealth of useful, updated information."
Library Journal

"When in doubt, consult WEDDLE's ... an industry standard."
Paula Santonocito
HRWIRE

" ...loads you up with pages and pages of ideas, Internet Recruiting ideas ... good ideas."
Mark Berger
The Fordyce Letter

"I think your service is great—the acknowledged leader in Internet guides for the industry!"
Tim Scheele, Chief Marketing Officer
NETSHARE. Inc.

"I picked up *WEDDLE's Guide to Employment Web-Sites* and want to recommend it to you ... he lists a lot of relevant information that I figure I can use to make determinations regarding which sites to use."
Scott Firth, President
DCI Technical Services

"I have a copy of *WEDDLE's Guide to Employment Web-Sites*, which I find very useful and time saving."
Anthony Clayton-Spray
CyberCable, France

"The *WEDDLE's 2001 Job Seeker's Guide to Employment Web Sites* supplies clear, completely current information about each site's services, features and fees—helping users instantly determine which site best meets their needs. If you are looking for an objective guide to employment websites, ExecuNet recommends *WEDDLE's Guide*."
ExecuNet, The Center for Executive Careers

" ... your newsletter is tremendously helpful to our recruiters. Keep up the fantastic work."
Shana Wiley
Harrahs

"Peter, half an hour ago, I read another one of your columns on cnnfn.com. I truly enjoy your columns. You cover the employment scene like no other. Hats off."
Rick Myers
President, Talent Zoo

"Just read an article by Mr. Weddle and was impressed with his insight into issues in recruiting in today's new world. I have been recruiting in corporate environments for about 20 years and haven't seen these issues addressed so effectively."

Randall D. Gregory
RDG Consulting

"It's been a couple of decades since I have had a need for a resume, and found your book insightful and most helpful. Thank you for taking the time to write it."

J.H., Canada

"I've just attended [Peter Weddle's] session and it was really great. Peter is giving new information I've never heard before and has some really helpful insights. ... Please pass my compliments on to Peter for sharing his expertise. Thanks!"

Marketing Manager
DBM

"Hi, I just went to your Web-site and was blown away by all the neat material. It is presented so well and is very compelling—I could hardly resist ordering ... !!!"

D.F., JobWhiz

"I found you book in the public library. Recently, I purchased my own copy from Amazon.com. It is a terrific book for breaking down the complexity of preparing resumes for the computer age. Thank you for writing this book."

R.M.

"Since the early beginnings of the Web, your site has been an inspiration to us and a 'real' source of practical advice in our business."

S. Y., JobsHawaii.com

"The program is excellent, very well thought out and the manual is extremely well done. Peter is just outstanding. I found it very useful."

President
Frank Palma Associates

"Good information for those who want to be the best of the best."

President
The RADS Group

"The information was extremely useful and can easily be applied to work procedures."

Recruiting Specialist
Administaff

"Just wanted you to know that ALL the participants rated today's program and presenter as excellent! You were informative, funny, and you put things into context so they could be easily understood. It was a terrific program!"

WEBS Career & Educational Counseling Service
Westchester County (NY) Library System

"Thank you for a very concise, logical and informative presentation today! I greatly appreciated your professionalism—there are enough 'screamers' out there!"

Executive Vice President
Lamay Associates

WEDDLE's

Directory
of
Employment-Related Internet Sites

for
← *Recruiters & Job Seekers* →

Directory n. 1. The address book of Internet sites that provide job boards, resume databases and other employment-related resources for recruiters and job seekers. 2. A comprehensive listing that (a) organizes employment-related Internet sites by category (e.g., occupational field, geographic focus) and (b) provides their online address for easy access.

2004

Special discounts on bulk quantities of WEDDLE's books are available
to corporations, professional associations and other organizations.
For details, please contact WEDDLE's at 203.964.1888 or visit our
Web-site at http://www.weddles.com.

FOR
Recruiters & Job Seekers everywhere

Men and Women
who face unprecedented challenges in the workplace
and
deserve the best resources available

Special thanks to Juliana Sciolla and Meagan Micozzi.

© 2004 Peter D. Weddle
All Rights Reserved.
Printed in the United States of America.

ISBN: 1-928734-19-7

This publication may not be reproduced, stored in a retrieval system
or transmitted in whole or in part, in any form or by any means, electronic,
mechanical, photocopying, recording, or otherwise, without the prior written
permission of WEDDLE's, 2052 Shippan Avenue, Stamford, CT 06902.

WEDDLE's
www.weddles.com
2052 Shippan Avenue
Stamford, CT 06902

Where People Matter Most

WEDDLE's Helping to Maximize Your ROI ... Your Return on the Internet

Table of Contents

	Page
Welcome Back!	8
About This Directory	9
What is WEDDLE's & Who is Peter Weddle?	11
WEDDLE's 2004 User's Choice Awards **Recruiters & Job Seekers Pick the Best Sites on the Web**	13
Site Categories & Index	15
WEDDLE's 2004 Web-Site Listings	19
WEDDLE's 2004 Catalog	309
for Job Seekers & Career Activists	310
for Recruiters & HR Professionals	313

> "a wealth of useful, updated information"
> *Library Journal*

Welcome Back!

Welcome to the 2004 edition of *WEDDLE's Directory of Employment-Related Internet Sites*. This is the fourth consecutive year that this Directory has been published. To those who have been with us since the beginning, we say "Welcome Back!" and to those who are using this resource for the first time, we hope that it serves you well.

As our "long-time" readers know, we update and publish this one-of-a-kind listing of employment-related Web-sites every year because the Internet is a dynamic, ever-changing environment. To make sure that the Directory works for you:

- We collect new sites, eliminate discontinued sites and revise site addresses that have changed. Typically, these revisions involve hundreds of potential destinations.
- In addition, we provide a continuous stream of updates throughout the year so that you are aware of site changes as soon as they occur. You can access this information free of charge at the WEDDLE's Web-site, www.weddles.com.

This year's edition lists over 7,500 sites, including many niche or specialty sites that are appearing in the Directory for the first time. In addition, it incorporates the significant changes that have occurred among older and more established sites due to consolidation and market changes. As a result, we think the 2004 edition of WEDDLE's Directory represents the single, most comprehensive and up-to-date roster of online resources available anywhere. And that makes it an especially powerful resource for recruiting great talent and for finding a new or better job.

In fact, whether you're a:

- Recruiter or Human Resource professional,
- Job Seeker or Career Activist,
- or both,

this Directory will put you on the Information Superhighway to career success. We hope you'll use it often and benefit greatly from that use

All the Best,
Peter Weddle
Stamford, CT

WEDDLE's is "… the gorilla of knowledge and Web-sites relating to getting a job, human resources and recruiting on the Internet!"
Recruiter
Stone Enterprises, Ltd

About This Directory

This Directory presents the Internet address (also called the Universal Resource Locator or URL) of Internet sites that provide employment-related services to recruiters and/or job seekers. To be included in the Directory, the site must post or fill jobs, post or distribute resumes, or provide recruitment support, career counseling and/or job search assistance over the Internet.

The Directory is designed to be used just as you would a traditional telephone directory. Sites are listed alphabetically by their name in one or more of three categories:

- **Occupational field** (e.g., engineering, finance and accounting, sales and marketing)
- **Industry** (e.g., banking, construction, healthcare, insurance)
- **Specialty** (e.g., bilingual professionals, diversity, military personnel transitioning into the private sector)

In addition, international sites and regional sites in the United States are organized by their specific geographic focus. For a complete list of the categories used in this Directory, please see the **Site Categories & Index** on Page 15.

How Can This Directory Help You?

There are over 40,000 employment-related sites currently operating on the Internet. Whether you're a recruiter, a job seeker or a person proactively managing your own career, you need to know your options in order to make the best use of these powerful resources. This Directory can help you do that. It will make sure that you don't overlook a site that can assist you and quickly identify those sites best able to address your specific situation or objective as well as their location on the Internet.

For example:

- If you're a recruiter who is looking for candidates to fill a senior level finance position located in California, you could check the listings under Finance (where you would find over 135 sites), Executive/Management (where you would find over 45 sites) and Regional-California (where you would find more than 65 sites).
- On the other hand, if you're a senior level financial executive who is living in California and interested in finding a new or better job, you could check the same listings and take advantage of the same sites to find that recruiter's opening and others posted online.

There's no guesswork, no slogging through thousands of unrelated listings on a search engine and no wandering around the Internet trying to find what you need by hit or miss. The Directory enables you to identify just the sites you need quickly and put their resources to work for you effectively. That's the way you maximize your ROI ... your return on the Internet.

A Word About Web-Site Addresses

A Web-site address or Universal Resource Locator (URL) typically includes two basic elements: <u>The root address</u> (e.g., the-name-of-the-site.com) and <u>extensions</u> which identify specific areas of the site. For example: (e.g., the-name-of-the-site.com/JobPostings.html or the-name-of-the-site.com/resumes).

When you select a Web-site to visit and enter its URL into your computer, remember the following rules:

- <u>In most cases, address extensions are case sensitive</u>. In other words, if the address that is listed in the Directory indicates that the extension includes one or more capital letters, make sure that you include them exactly as shown in the address.

- <u>Unfortunately, extensions often change</u>. The best Web-site operators are continuously updating and improving their sites, and when they do, they often change the extensions to reflect their changes. How can you still use the address if the extensions listed in the Directory don't seem to work? Use a technique called "peeling." This technique involves eliminating, one at a time, each of the extensions between the forward slashes in an address, beginning with the last extension, until the Web-site opens. Then, look for links on the open page to find that area of the site you are trying to reach.

   For example, the Directory might list the following address for a site you want to visit: www.the-name-of-the-site.com/adposts/jobs/newposts.html. If you enter that address into your computer and the site doesn't open (or you get an error message), then peel back the last extension (newposts.html) and try again. If the site still doesn't open, peel back the next extension (jobs) and try again. Continue this process, until the site opens and then look for a link to the area of the site of interest to you. When you click on that link, note the new address that appears on your computer tool bar. Record that address on the Notes page of your Directory so that it will be readily available the next time you want to visit the site.

Keeping Our Information Up-to-Date

WEDDLE's makes every effort to keep the information it publishes current and up-to-date. The Internet, however, is always changing, and WEDDLE's is always seeking updates and corrections to its listings. If you find a discrepancy, please notify us at 203.964.1888 or on the Internet at publisher@weddles.com. We appreciate your assistance and pay careful attention to what you tell us.

Whenever we become aware of a change or discrepancy, we contact the appropriate site, obtain the correct information and then publish it on our Web-site for you and others to see. So, **log onto www.weddles.com regularly** and click on the link entitled Free Book Updates on our toolbar. It's the best way to stay on top of the ever-changing universe of helpful employment resources on the Internet.

WEDDLE's Helping to Maximize Your ROI ... Your Return on the Internet

What is WEDDLE's & Who is Peter Weddle?

What is WEDDLE's?

WEDDLE's is a research, publishing, consulting and training firm specializing in HR leadership, employment, job search and personal career management.

- Since 1996, WEDDLE's has conducted groundbreaking surveys of:
  - recruiters and job seekers on the Internet, and
  - Web-sites providing employment-related services.

  Its findings and research have been cited in such publications as *The Wall Street Journal*, *The New York Times*, and in *Money*, *Fortune*, and *Inc.* magazines.

- WEDDLE's publishes books, guides and directories that focus on companies' acquisition and leadership of human capital and on individuals' achievement of their employment and career goals.

  For recruiters and HR professionals, its publications include:

  - *WEDDLE's Newsletter for Recruiters & HR Professionals* **[FREE]**
  - *WEDDLE's 2004 Guide to Employment Web Sites, The Recruiter's Edition* **[UPDATED]**
  - *WEDDLE's 2004 Directory of Employment-Related Internet Sites For Recruiters & Job Seekers* **[UPDATED]**
  - *Postcards From Space: Being the Best in Online Recruitment & HR Management*
  - *WEDDLE's Recruiter's Guide to Association Web Sites*
  - *Generalship: HR Leadership in a Time of War* **[NEW]**
  - *Extreme HR: Pushing the Envelope to World Class HR Performance* **[NEW]**
  - *The Keys to Successful Recruiting and Staffing* **[NEW]**

  For job seekers and career activists, its publications include:

  - *WEDDLE's Newsletter for Job Seekers & Career Activists* **[FREE]**
  - *WEDDLE's 2004 Guide to Employment Web Sites, The Job Seeker's Edition* **[UPDATED]**
  - *WEDDLE's 2004 Directory of Employment-Related Internet Sites For Recruiters & Job Seekers* **[UPDATED]**
  - *WEDDLE's InfoNotes (WIN) Writing a Great Resume*
  - *WizNotes: Fast Guides to Job Boards & Career Portals* **[NEW]** *Engineering, Sales & Marketing, Associations and others*
  - *CliffsNotes: Finding a Job on the Web*

- WEDDLE's provides consultation to organizations in the areas of:
  - HR leadership;
  - human capital formation;
  - recruitment strategy formulation;
  - employment brand development and positioning;
  - recruitment process re-engineering and optimization;
  - Web-site design, development and implementation;
  - employee retention and performance enhancement strategies;
  - selection, installation and use of HR/staffing metrics; and
  - other topics central to effective staffing and HR management.

- WEDDLE's delivers private seminars and workshops designed to train recruiters and recruitment managers in the Best Practices and Best Policies of Internet recruiting. Each session is tailored to the specific competency level of participants (be they desk recruiters or CEO's) and the mission of their organization (corporate employer, staffing firm, advertising agency or search firm).

Who is Peter Weddle?

WEDDLE's publications and services were created by Peter Weddle, a former recruiter and business CEO turned author and speaker. He writes a weekly column about Internet recruiting and HR management for CareerJournal.com from *The Wall Street Journal* and two bi-weekly newsletters (one for recruiters and HR professionals, the other for job seekers and career activists) that are distributed worldwide. Weddle has also authored or edited almost twenty books—including *Generalship: HR Leadership in a Time of War, Extreme HR: Pushing the Envelope to World Class Performance, Career Fitness, WEDDLE's InfoNotes (WIN): Writing a Great Resume*, and *CliffsNotes: Finding a Job on the Web*—and written numerous articles for leading magazines and journals. He has been cited in *The New York Times, The Washington Post, The Boston Globe, U.S. News & World Report, The Wall Street Journal, USA Today* and numerous other publications and has spoken to trade and professional associations and corporate meetings all over the world.

"The WEDDLE's Seminar has been held in cities around the country to rave reviews; in fact, more than 95% have said they found the seminars to both very informative and very helpful."
CareerJournal.com
from The Wall Street Journal

WEDDLE's Helping to Maximize Your ROI ... Your Return on the Internet

User's Choice Awards

Recruiter's & Job Seekers Pick the Best Sites on the Web

Who offers the best advice on which employment sites are most helpful to recruiters and job seekers? We think the answer to that question is obvious ... it's you, the recruiters and job seekers who have used the sites. And that's what the **WEDDLE's User's Choice Awards** are all about. It's your chance to:

- recognize the Web-sites that provide the best level of service and value to their visitors, and
- help others make best use of the employment resources online.

For more information about the Awards and to cast your vote for the 2005 User's Choice Awards, please visit the WEDDLE's site at www.weddles.com and click on the Online Poll button on our Home Page.

> **WEDDLE's 2004 User's Choice Awards
> are sponsored by Bernard Hodes Group.**

The 2004 Winners

This year's winning sites received the most votes from among thousands of ballots cast by job seekers and recruiters between January and December, 2003. Those who cast ballots were able to select sites from a list provided by WEDDLE's or write-in their own winners.

In previous years, WEDDLE's User's Choice Awards were presented to both general purpose and specialty sites in the following categories:

- Best overall,
- Best customer service for recruiters,
- Best information for job seekers,
- Most "recruiter friendly" and
- Most "job seeker friendly."

General purpose sites were defined to be Internet destinations that support employment activities for all professions, crafts, trades and industries without regard to geographic location. Specialty sites were defined to be Internet destinations that support employment activities for a specific occupational field, industry, geographic location or some combination of those factors.

The popularity of the Awards, however, has meant that both the number of voters and the sites for which they cast ballots have increased significantly. That being the case, it seemed both timely and appropriate to increase the number of winners. Therefore, WEDDLE's User's Choice Awards will now recognize the top thirty sites that receive the most votes from both job seekers and recruiters. These sites represent the elite of online job boards and career portals, according to the users who put their services to work. There is no higher accolade, and WEDDLE's congratulates each and all of the sites on their accomplishment.

WEDDLE's 2004 User's Choice Awards
The Elite of the Online Employment Industry

America's Job Bank	HRJobs (SHRM.org)
Best Jobs USA	IEEE Job Site
The Blue Line	JobsinME.com
CareerBuilder.com	jobsinthemoney.com
CareerJournal.com	Legal Career Center Network
ComputerJobs.com	Medzilla
Computerwork.com	Monster.com
ConstructionJobs.com	NationJob.com
Craigslist	Net-Temps
DICE	RegionalHelpWanted.com
EmploymentGuide.com	techies.com
ExecuNet	TrueCareers
FlipDog.com	Vault.com
Hcareers	VetJobs.com
HotJobs.com	Workopolis

WEDDLE's Helping to Maximize Your ROI ... Your Return on the Internet

Site Categories & Index

This section contains an alphabetical listing of all of the categories under which employment-related sites are listed in the Directory. To find a specific category's location in the Directory, check its page number listed in the Index below. Sites are listed alphabetically in a category by their name (which may not be their URL or Internet address).

Page

— A —

Administrative/Clerical/Secretarial (see also Classifieds)	19
Advertising	19
Agriculture	21
Archeology/Anthropology	21
Architecture	21
Arts	21
Association-Professional & Trade/Affinity Group	23
Astronomy	39
Automotive	39
Aviation	41

— B —

Banking	41
Bilingual Professionals	43
Biology/Biotechnology	43
Building Industry	47
Business	47

— C —

Call Center	51
Career Counseling/Job Search Services	53
Chemistry	55
Child & Elder Care	55
Classifieds-Newspaper	55
College/Internships/Entry Level/Graduate School Graduates	71
Computer-Aided Design, Manufacturing & Engineering	77
Construction (see also Engineering)	77
Consultants	79
Contract Employment/Part Time Employment (see also Search Firms)	79
Culinary/Food Preparation (see also Hospitality)	81

— D —

Data Processing	83
Dental	83
Diversity	83

Site Categories & Index (continued)

Page

— E —

Economists	89
Education/Academia	91
Engineering	95
Entertainment/Acting	101
Environmental	103
Equipment Leasing	105
Executive/Management	105

— F —

Fashion	107
Feminism	107
Fiber Optics	107
Finance & Accounting (see also Banking, Insurance)	109
Funeral Industry	115

— G —

Gaming	117
General	117
Graphic Arts/Electronic & Traditional	129

— H —

Healthcare/Medical	131
High Tech/Technical/Technology	147
Hospitality (see also Culinary/Food Preparation)	147
Hourly (see also Classifieds-Newspaper) **[NEW]**	149
Human Resources	149

— I —

Industrial/Manufacturing	155
Information Technology/Information Systems	157
Insurance	175
International	177
Investment/Brokerage	203

— J —

Job Fairs Online	203
Journalism & Media (see also Graphic Arts)	203

— L —

Law	205
Law Enforcement	209

Site Categories & Index (continued)

Page

— L (continued) —

Library & Information Science	209
Linguistics	209
Logistics	209

— M —

Military Personnel Transitioning into the Private Sector	211
Modeling [NEW]	211
Music	211

— N —

Non-Profit	213

— O —

Outdoors/Recreation/Sports	213

— P —

Packaging for Food & Drug	215
Pharmaceutical	215
Physics	217
Printing & Bookbinding	219
Public Sector/Government	219
Publishing	221
Purchasing	221

— Q —

Quality/Quality Control	221

— R —

Real Estate	221
Recruiters Resources	223
Recruitment Advertising-Non-Newspaper Print & Online	229
Regional-USA	231
Religion	283
Retail	285

— S —

Sales & Marketing	285
Science/Scientists	289
Search Firms/Staffing Agencies/Recruiters	295
Social Service	299
Statistical	299

Site Categories & Index (continued)

Page

— T —

Telecommunications	301
Telecommuting	301
Trade Organizations	301
Training	303
Transportation	305

— V —

Volunteer Positions	305

-Y-

Young Adult/Teen Positions	307

ORDER NOW & SAVE MONEY

☛ Order your 2005 editions of WEDDLE's books <u>right now</u>, and you'll save money.

Order the 2005 Recruiter's Guide to Employment Web Sites ...
- by June 1, 2004, and save $5.00 on the purchase price. (from $27.95 to $22.95)
- by September 1, 2004, and save $3.00 on the purchase price. (from $27.95 to $24.95)
- by October 1, 2004, and you save $2.00 on the purchase price. (from $27.95 to $25.95)

Order the 2005 Directory of Employment-Related Internet Sites ...
- by June 1, 2004, and save $8.00 on the purchase price. (from $49.95 to $41.95)
- by September 1, 2004, and save $5.00 on the purchase price. (from $49.95 to $44.95)
- by October 1, 2004, and you save $3.00 on the purchase price. (from $49.95 to $46.95)

To order, please call 203.964.1888

WEDDLE's Helping to Maximize Your ROI ... Your Return on the Internet

WEDDLE's
2004 Directory of Internet Addresses
for Employment-Related Sites

All addresses in this Directory were obtained from public sources.
Some addresses may have changed since publication of the Directory.
WEDDLE's 2052 Shippan Avenue, Stamford, CT 06902 All rights reserved.

■ Indicates 2004 WEDDLE's User's Choice Award Winner

-A-

Administrative/Clerical/Secretarial (see also Classifieds)

Administrative Resource Network	www.adresnet.com/jobs.html
iHireMedicalSecretaries.com	www.ihiremedicalsecretaries.com
iHireSecretarial.com	www.ihiresecretarial.com
MyOwnVA.com [United Kingdom]	www.myownva.com
National Association of Executive Secretaries and Administrative Assistants	www.naesaa.com/verifjb.asp
ReceptionistJobStore.com	www.receptionistjobstore.com
SecretaryJobStore	www.secretaryjobstore.com
SecsInTheCity [United Kingdom]	www.secsinthecity.co.uk
VirtualAssistants.com	www.virtualassistants.com

Advertising

NationJob Network-Advertising & Media Jobs Page	www.nationjob.com/media
Adweek	www.adweek.com/aw/classifieds/index.jsp
The American Advertising Federation	www.aaf.org/jobs/index.html
The Association for Interactive Marketing Career Center	www.interactivehq.org/industry/careers.asp
Association of National Advertisers Job Opportunities	www.ana.net/hr/hr.htm
Communicators & Marketers Jobline	http://cmjobline.org
MediaRecruiter.com	www.mediarecruiter.com
Promotion Marketing Association Job Bank	www.pmalink.org/resources/careers.asp
TalentZoo.com	www.talentzoo.com
Television Bureau of Advertising	www.tvb.org/jobcenter/index.html
Work in PR	www.workinpr.com

Notes
Favorite sites, useful resources

WEDDLE's Helping to Maximize Your ROI ... Your Return on the Internet

Agriculture

Ag Jobs USA	www.agjobsusa.com
Agricultural Employment in British Columbia	www.island.net/~awpb/emop/startag.html
American Agricultural Economic Association Employment Service	www.aaea.org/classifieds
American Society of Agricultural Engineering	www.asae.org/membership/career.html
American Society of Agronomy	www.asa-cssa-sssa.org/career
American Society of Animal Science	www.asas.org
American Society of Horticultural Science HortOpportunities	www.ashs.org/careers.html
California Agricultural Technical Institute ATI-Net	www.atinet.org/jobs.asp
Dairy Network Career Center	www.dairynetwork.com
Farms.com	www.farms.com/calssifieds/index.cfm
Texas A&M Poultry Science Department	http://gallus.tamu.edu/Jobs/Industry/Poultrypositions.htm
Weed Science Society of America WeedJobs: Positions in Weed Science	www.wssa.net/weedjobs

Archeology/Anthropology

American Anthropology Association	www.aaanet.org/careers.htm
Society for American Archeology Careers, Opportunities & Jobs	www.saa.org/careers/index.html
Southwest Archeology	www.swanet.org/jobs.html

Architecture

AEC Job Bank	www.aecjobbank.com
American Institute of Architects Online	www.aia.org/careercenter/default.asp
ArchitectJobs.com	www.architectjobs.com
Environmental Construction Engineering Architectural Jobs Online	www.eceajobs.com

Arts

ArtJob Online	www.artjob.org
Art Libraries Society of North America JobNet	http://arlisna.org/jobs.html
ArtNetwork	http://artmarketing.com
The Arts Deadline List	www.xensei.com/adl
Freelancers/TalentX	www.talentx.com
New York Foundation for the Arts	www.nyfa.org/opportunities.asp?type=Job&id=94&fid=6&sid=17

Notes
Favorite sites, useful resources

Association-Professional & Trade/Affinity Group

Academic Physician & Scientist	www.acphysci.com/aps.htm
AcademyHealth	www.academyhealth.org
Academy of Managed Care Pharmacy	www.amcp.org
The Advanced Computing Systems Association	www.usenix.org
Air & Waste Management Association	www.awma.org/resources/career
American Academy of Otolaryngology-Head & Neck Surgery	www.entnet.org/careers
American Academy of Pharmaceutical Physicians	www.aapp.org
American Accounting Association Web Placement Service	http://aaahq.org/placements/default.cfm
The American Advertising Federation	www.aaf.org/jobs/index.html
American Agricultural Economic Association Employment Service	www.aaea.org/classifieds
American Anthropology Association	www.aaanet.org/careers.htm
American Association of Brewing Chemists	www.asbcnet.org/SERVICES/career.htm
American Association for Budget and Program Analysis	www.aabpa.org/employ.html
American Association of Cereal Chemists	www.aaccnet.org/membership/careerplacement.asp
American Association for Clinical Chemistry	www.aacc.org
American Association of Critical Care Nurses	www.aacn.org
American Association of Finance & Accounting	www.aafa.com/career.htm
American Association of Law Libraries Job Placement Hotline	www.aallnet.org/hotline
American Association of Medical Assistants	www.aama-ntl.org
American Association of Pharmaceutical Scientists	www.aaps.pharmaceutica.com/careerCenter/job_listing.asp
American Association of Respiratory Care	www.aarc.org
American Astronomical Society Job Register	www.aas.org/JobRegister/index.html
American Bankers Association	http://aba.careerbank.com
American Chemical Society cen-chemjobs.org	www.cen-chemjobs.com
American College of Clinical Pharmacology	www.aoop1.org
American College of Clinical Pharmacy	www.accp.com
American College of Healthcare Executives Employment Service	www.ache.org
American College of Occupational and Environmental Medicine	www.acoem.org
American Dental Hygienists' Association	www.adha.org/careerinfo/index.html
American Design Drafting Association	www.adda.org

Notes
Favorite sites, useful resources

Association-Professional & Trade/Affinity Group (continued)

American Educational Research Association Job Openings	http://aera.net/jobposts/default.asp
American Evaluation Associaton	www.eval.org/JobBank/jobbank.htm
American Foundation for the Blind AFB Career Connect	www.afb.org/CareerConnect/users/careers.asp
American Industrial Hygiene Association	www.aiha.org/Employment Service/html/employmentservicehome.htm
American Institute of Architects Online	www.aia.org/careercenter/default.asp
American Institute of Biological Sciences	www.aibs.org
American Institute of Certified Public Accountants Career Center	www.cpa2biz.com/Career/default.htm
American Institute of Chemical Engineers Career Services	www.aiche.org/careers
American Institute of Graphic Arts	www.aiga.org
American Institute of Physics Career Services	www.aip.org/industry.html
American Library Association Library Education and Employment Menu Page	www.ala.org/education
American Marketing Association Career Center	www.marketingpower.com/live/content.php?Item_ID=966
American Medical Association Journal of the AMA (JAMA) Physician Recruitment Ads	www.ama-assn.org/cgi-bin/webad
American Meteorological Society Employment Announcements	www.ametsoc.org
American Nurses Association	www.nursingworld.org
American Occupational Therapy Association	www.aota.org
American Pharaceutical Association	www.aphanet.org
American Physical Society	www.aps.org/jobs
American Physical Therapy Association	www.apta.org
American Psychological Association Online PsycCareers	www.psyccareers.com
American Psychological Society Observer Job Listings	www.psychologicalscience.org/jobs
American Society of Agricultural Engineering	www.asae.org/membership/career.html
American Society of Agronomy	www.asa-cssa-sssa.org/career
American Society of Animal Science	www.fass.org/job.asp
American Society of Association Executives Career Headquarters	www.asaenet.org/careers
American Society for Cell Biology	www.ascb.org
American Society for Clinical Laboratory Science	www.ascls.org
American Society for Clinical Pathology	www.ascp.org

Notes
Favorite sites, useful resources

Association-Professional & Trade/Affinity Group (continued)

American Society of Clinical Pharmacology and Therapeutics	www.ascpt.org
American Society of Gene Therapy	www.asgt.org
American Society of Horticultural Science HortOpportunities	www.ashs.org/careers.html
American Society of Interior Designers Job Bank	www.asid.org/career_center/job_opp/job.asp
American Society of Mechanical Engineers Career Center	www.asme.org/jobs
American Society for Microbiology	www.asm.org
American Society of Pharmacognosy	www.phcog.org
American Society for Training & Development Job Bank	http://jobs.astd.org
American Society of Women Accountants Employment Opportunities	www.aswa.org/wanted.html
American Speech-Language Hearing Association Online Career Center	www.asha.org/about/career
American Statistical Association Statistics Career Center	www.amstat.org/careers
American Veterinary Medical Association Career Center	http://jobs.avma.org
American Water Works Association Career Center (Water Jobs)	www.awwa.org
Arizona Hospital and Healthcare Association AZHealthJobs	www.azhha.org
Art Libraries Society of North America JobNet	http://arlisna.org/jobs.html
Association for Applied Human Pharmacology [Germany]	www.agah-web.de
Association of Career Professionals International	www.iacmp.org
Association of Certified Fraud Examiners Career Center	www.cfenet.com services/career.asp
Association of Clinical Research in the Pharmaceutical Industry [United Kingdom]	www.acrpi.com
Association of Clinical Reseach Professionals Career Center	www.acrpnet.org
Association for Computing Machinery Career Resource Center	http://career.acm.org/crc
Association for Educational Communications and Technology Job Center	www.aect.org
Association of ex-Lotus Employees	www.axle.org/careerframeset.html
Association of Finance Professionals Career Services	www.afponline.org/careerservices
Association of Graduate Careers Advisory Service [United Kingdom]	www.agcas.org.uk

Notes
Favorite sites, useful resources

Association-Professional & Trade/Affinity Group (continued)

The Association for Institutional Research	www.airweb.org/page.asp?page=2
The Association for Interactive Marketing Career Center	www.interactivehq.org/industry/careers.asp
Association of Internet Professionals National Job Board	www.association.org
Association of Latino Professionals in Finance & Accounting Job Postings	www.alpfa.org/professi/careoppo.asp
Association of Legal Information Systems Managers Job Listings	www.alism.org/jobs.htm
Association of National Advertisers Job Opportunities	www.ana.net/hr/hr.htm
Association of Perioperative Registered Nurses Online Career Center	www.aorn.org/Careers/default.htm
Association of Teachers of Technical Writing	www.attw.org
Association for Women in Computing	www.awc-hq.org
Bank Administration Institute	www.bai.org
Bank Marketing Association	www.bmanet.org
Bay Area Bioscience Center	www.bayareabioscience.org
Biomedical Engineering Society	www.bmes.org
Biotechnology Association of Alabama	www.bioalabama.org
Biotechnology Association of Maine	www.mainebiotech.org
Biotechnology Council of New Jersey	www.newjerseybiotech.org
Black Data Processing Association Online	www.bdpa.org
Biotechnology Association of Alabama	www.bioalabama.com
Board of Pharmaceutical Specialties	www.bpsweb.org
Business Marketing Association	www.marketing.org
California Agricultural Technical Institute ATI-Net AgJobs	www.atinet.org/jobs.asp
California Dental Hygienists' Association Employment Opportunities	www.cdha.org/advertising/adpage.html
California Mortgage Brokers Association Career Center	www.cambweb.org
California Separation Science Society	www.casss,org
Canadian Society of Biochemistry and Mollecular and Cellular Biologists Experimental Medicine Job Listing	www.medcor.mcglll.ca/EXPMED/DOCS/jobs.html
Capital Markets Credit Analysts Society Resume Service	www.cmcas.org/resumeservice.asp
College and University Personnel Association JobLine	www.cupa.org/jobline/jobline.htm
Colorado Health and Hospital Association	www.cha.com
Computing Research Association Job Announcements	www.cra.org/jobs/main/cra.jobs.html
Controlled Release Society	www.controlledrelease.org

Notes
Favorite sites, useful resources

Association-Professional & Trade/Affinity Group (continued)

Council for Advancement & Support of Education Jobs Online	www.case.org/jobs
Design Management Institute Job Bank	www.designmgt.org/dmi/html/jobbank/jobbank_d.jsp
Digital Printing and Imaging Association Employment Exchange (with the Screenprinting & Graphic Imaging Association International)	www.sgia.org/employ/employ.html
Drilling Research Institute Classifieds	www.drillers.com/classifieds.cfm
Drug Information Association Employment Opportunities	www.diahome.org/docs/Jobs/Jobs_index.cfm
Financial Executives Institute Career Center	www.fei.org/careers
Financial Management Association International Placement Services	www.fma.org/2003placement
Financial Managers Society Career Center	www.fmsinc.org/cms/?pid=1025
Financial Women International Careers	www.fwi.org/careers/career.htm
Global Association of Risk Professionals Career Center	www.garp.com/careercenter/index.asp
Georgia Association of Personnel Services	www.jobconnection.com
Georgia Pharmacy Association	www.gpha.org
Graphic Artists Guild JobLine	www.gag.org/jobline/index.html
HTML Writers Guild HWG-Jobs	www.hwg.org/lists/hwg-jobs
Human Resource Association of the National Capital Area Job Bank Listing	http://hra-nca.org/job_list.asp
Human Resource Independent Consultants (HRIC) On-Line Job Leads	www.hric.org/hric/hrcaopp1.html
Human Resource Management Association of Mid Michigan Job Postings	http://hrmamm.com/jobs.asp
Institute of Electrical & Electronics Engineers Job Site	www.ieee.org/jobs
Institute of Food Science & Technology	www.ifst.org
Institute of Internal Auditors Online Audit Career Center	www.theiia.org/careercenter/index.cfm
Institute of Management Accountants Career Center	www.imanet.org/ima/ sec.asp?TRACKID=&CID=12&DID=12
Institute of Management and Administration's Supersite	www.ioma.com
Institute of Real Estate Management Jobs Bulletin	www.irem.org/i06_ind_roc/html/post.html
Institute for Supply Management Career Center	www.ism.ws/CareerCenter/index.cfm
The Instrumentation, Systems and Automation Society Online ISA Jobs	www.isa.org/isa_es
International Association of Business Communicators Career Centre	www.iabc.com

Notes
Favorite sites, useful resources

WEDDLE's Helping to Maximize Your ROI ... Your Return on the Internet

Association-Professional & Trade/Affinity Group (continued)

International Association of Conference Centers Online (North America)	www.iaccnorthamerica.org/resources/index.cfm?fuseaction=JobBoard
International Association for Human Resource Information Management Job Central	http://ihr.hrdpt.com
International Customer Service Association Job Board	http://secure2.neology.com/ICSA/jobs/employer/welcome.cfm
International Foundation of Employee Benefit Plans Job Postings	www.ifebp.org/jobs/default.asp
Independent Human Resource Consultants Association	www.ihrca.com/Contract_Regular.asp
International Society for Molecular Plant-Microbe Interactions	www.ismpinet.org/career
International Society for Performance Improvement Job Bank	www.ispi.org
Iowa Biotechnology Association	www.iowabiotech.org
Maryland Association of CPAs Job Connect	www.macpa.org/services/jobconnt/index.htm
Massachusetts Biotechnology Council	www.massbio.org
MdBio, Inc. (Maryland Bioscience)	www.mdbio.org
Media Communications Association International Job Hotline	www.itva.org/resources/job_hotline.htm
Media Human Resource Association	www.shrm.org/mhra/index.asp
Medical Marketing Association	www.mmanet.org
Metroplex Association of Personnel Consultants	www.recruitingfirms.com
MichBIO	www.michbio.org
Michigan Pharmacists Association	www.mipharm.com
The Minerals, Metals, Materials Society JOM	www.tms.org/pubs/journals/JOM/classifieds.html
Missouri Pharmacy Association	www.morx.com
Music Library Association Job Placement	www.music.indiana.edu/Som/placement/index.html
National Association of Black Accountants, Inc. Career Center	www.nabainc.jobcontrolcenter.com
National Association of Boards of Pharmacy	www.nabp.net
National Association for College Admission Counseling Career Opportunities	www.nacac.com/olaccifieds.cfm
National Association of Colleges & Employers (NACE)	www.nacelink.com
National Association for Female Executives	www.nafe.com
National Association of Hispanic Nurses Houston Chapter	www.nahnhouston.org
National Association for Printing Leadership	www.napl.org
National Association of Printing Ink Manufacturers	www.napim.org

Notes
Favorite sites, useful resources

Association-Professional & Trade/Affinity Group (continued)

National Association of Sales Professionals Career Center	www.nasp.com
National Association of School Psychologists	www.naspcareercenter.org
National Association of Securities Professionals Current Openings	www.nasphq.com/career.html
National Association of Securities Professionals (Atlanta) Current Openings	www.naspatlanta.com/career.html
National Association of Securities Professionals (New York) Underground Railroad	www.nasp-ny.org
National Association of Social Workers Joblink	www.socialworkers.org/joblinks/default.asp
National Community Pharmacists Association Independent Pharmacy Matching Service	www.ncpanet.org/management/ipms.shtml
National Contract Management Association	www.ncmajobcontrolcenter.com
National Council on Compensation Insurance Careers	www.ncci.com/ncciweb/ncci.asp?If=control_panel.asp&mf=/ncci research/careers/careers.htm
National Environmental Health Association	www.neha.org
National Federation of Paralegal Associations Career Center	www.paralegals.org/Center/home.html
National Field Selling Association	www.nfsa.com
National Fire Prevention Association Online Career Center	www.nfpa.org/catalog/home/CareerCenter/index.asp
National Funeral Directors Association	www.nfda.org
National Insurance Recruiters Association Online Job Database	www.nirassn.com/positions.cfm
National Network of Commercial Real Estate Women Job Bank	www.nncrew.org/job_bank/job_bank_introduction_frm.html
National Organization for Professional Advancement of Black Chemists and Chemical Engineers University of Michigan Chapter	www.engin.umich.edu/soc/nobcche
National Society of Black Engineers	www.nsbe.org
National Society of Collegiate Scholars Career Connection	www.nscs.org/CareerConnections/Index.cfm
National Society of Hispanic MBAs Career Center	www.nshmba.org
National Society of Professional Engineers Employment	www.nspe.org/em-home.asp
National Venture Capital Association	www.nvca.org
National Weather Association Job Corner	www.nwas.org/jobs.html
National Writer's Union Job Hotline	www.nwu.org/hotline/index.html
The New York Biotechnology Association	www.nyba.org
New York New Media Association	www.nynma.org
New York Society of Security Analysts Career Resources	www.nyssa.org/jobs

Notes
Favorite sites, useful resources

WEDDLE's Helping to Maximize Your ROI ... Your Return on the Internet

Association-Professional & Trade/Affinity Group (continued)

Northeast Human Resource Association Career Center	www.nehra.com/career.php?PHPSESSID=3370132aae438e135227dc62b488025c
Oregon Bioscience Association	www.oregon-bioscience.com
Petroleum Services Association of Canada Employment	www.psac.ca
Professionals in Human Resource Association Career Center	www.pihra.org/capirasn/careers.nsf/home?open
Project Management Institute Career Headquarters	www.pmi.org/CareerHQ
Promotion Marketing Association Job Bank	www.pmalink.org/resources/careers.asp
Radiological Society of North America	www.rsna.org
Risk & Insurance Management Society Careers	www.rims.org/Template.cfm?Section=JobBank1&Template=/Jobbank/SearchJobForm.cfm
Sales & Marketing Executives International Career Center	www.smei.org/careers/index.shtml
Screenprinting & Graphic Imaging Association International	www.sgia.org/employ/employ.html
Securities Industry Association Career Resource Center	www.sia.com/career
Sheet Metal and Air Conditioning Contractor's Association	www.smacna.org
Society for American Archeology Careers, Opportunities & Jobs	www.saa.org/careers/index.html
Society of Automotive Engineers Job Board	www.sae.org/careers/recrutad.htm
Society of Competitive Intelligence Professionals Job Marketplace	www.scip.org/jobs/index.asp
Society of Hispanic Professional Engineers Career Services	www.shpe.org
⚐ Society for Human Resource Management HRJobs	www.shrm.org/jobs
Society for Industrial & Organizational Psychology JobNet	www.siop.org/JobNet
Society of Petrologists & Well Log Analysts Job Opportunities	www.spwla.org
Society of Risk Analysis Opportunities	www.sra.org/opptys.php
Society of Satellite Professionals International Career Center	www.sspi.broadbandcareers.com/Default.asp
Society of Women Engineers Career Services	www.societyofwomenengineers.org/specialservices/careerservices.aspx

Notes
Favorite sites, useful resources

Association-Professional & Trade/Affinity Group (continued)

SPIE Web-International Society for Optical Engineering	www.spieworks.com
Strategic Account Management Association Career Resources	www.strategicaccounts.com/ public/career/index.asp
Student Conservation Association	www.thesca.org
Teachers of English to Speakers of Other Languages Job Finder	www.tesol.org
Technical Association of the Pulp & Paper Industry Jobline	www.tappi.org/index.asp? ip=-1&ch=14&rc=-1
Telecommunication Industry Association Online	www.tiaonline.org
Texas Healthcare & Bioscience Institute	www.thbi.org
Utah Life Sciences Association	www.utahlifescience.com
Virginia Biotechnology Association	www.vabio.org
Washington Biotechnology & Biomedical Association	www.wabio.com
Weed Science Society of America WeedJobs: Positions in Weed Science	www.wssa.net/weedjobs
Wisconsin Biotechnology Association	www.wisconsinbiotech.org
Women in Technology	www.worldWIT.org
Women in Technology International (WITI) 4Hire	www.witi4hire.com

Astronomy

American Astronomical Society Job Register	www.aas.org/JobRegister
Board of Physics & Astronomy	www.nas.edu/bpa

Automotive

Autocareers	www.autocareers.com
Auto Head Hunter	www.autoheadhunter.net
AutoJobs.com	www.autodealerjobs.com
Auto Techs USA	www.autotechsusa.com
Auto Town	www.autotown.com
Auto Jobs	www.autodealerjobs.com
Auto Tech USA	www.autotechusa.com
Automotive Aftermarket Jobs	www.ouctomtrucks.net
AutomotiveTechs.com	www.automotivetechs.com
Car Careers	www.carcareers.com
CarDealerJobs.com	www.cardealerjobs.com
Motor Careers	www.motorcareers.com
Need Techs.com	www.needtechs.com
Racing Jobs	www.racingjobs.com

Find Great Talent. ← WEDDLE's 2004 Recruiter's Guide

Notes
Favorite sites, useful resources

Aviation

Aeroindustryjobs	www.aeroindustryjobs.com
Aerospace Jobs	http://hometown.aol.com/aerojobs
AVCrew.com	www.avcrew.com
Aviation Employment	www.aviationemployment.com
Aviation Employment NOW	www.aenworld.com
Aviation Employment Placement Service	www.aeps.com
AviationJobSearch.com	www.aviationjobsearch.com
Aviation World Services	www.aviationworldservices.com
AVJobs.com	www.avjobs.com
Careers in Aviation	www.aec.net
Federal Aviation Administration	http://ftp.tc.faa.gov/avi_edu/coop/Resumes
Find A Pilot	www.findapilot.com
FliteJobs.com	www.flitejobs.com
Just Helicopters	www.justhelicopters.com
Landings	www.landings.com
The Mechanic	www.the-mechanic.com/jobs.html
NationJob Network-Aviation	www.nationjob.com/aviation
Pilot Jobs	www.pilot-jobs.com
Space Careers	www.spacelinks.com/spacecareers

-B-

Banking

American Banker Online Career Zone	www.americanbanker.com/careerzone
American Bankers Association	www.aba.com
Argus Clearinghouse	www.clearinghouse.net/index.html
Bank Administration Institute	www.bai.org
Bank Info	www.bankinfo.com
Bank Jobs	www.bankjobs.com
Bank Marketing Association	www.bmanet.org
BankingBoard.com	www.bankingboard.com
Banking Job Site	www.bankingjobsite.com
Banking Job Store	www.bankingjobstore.com
BanksHiringOnline.com	http://banks.hiringonline.com
CareerBank.com	www.careerbank.com
CreditCardJobs.net	www.creditcardjobs.net
Financial Job Network	www.fjn.com

Notes
Favorite sites, useful resources

Banking (continued)

FINANCIALjobs.com	www.financialjobs.com
Financial Women International Careers	www.fwi.org/careers/career.htm
The Finance Beat	http://business.searchbeat.com/finance.htm
Florida Bankers Association	www.fba.careersite.com
GTNews [United Kingdom]	www.gtnews.com
iHireBanking.com	www.ihirebanking.com
The Investment Management and Trust Exchange	http://kempcon.com
Loan Closer Jobs	www.loancloserjobs.com
LoanOfficerJobs.com	www.loanofficerjobs.com
Loan Originator Jobs	www.loanoriginatorjobs.com
LoanProcessorJobs.com	www.loanprocessorjobs.com
LoanServicingJobs.com	www.loanservicingjobs.com
Mortgage Job Store	www.mortgagejobstore.com
National Banking Network	www.nbn-jobs.com
Real Estate Finance Jobs	www.realestatefinancejobs.com
Society of Risk Analysis Opportunities	www.sra.org/opptys.php
TitleBoard.com	www.titleboard.com

Bilingual Professionals

Asia-Net	www.asia-net.com
Bilingual-Jobs	www.bilingual-jobs.com
CHALLENGEUSA	www.challengeusa.com
Eflweb	www.eflweb.com
Euroleaders	www.euroleaders.com
Hispanic Chamber of Commerce JobCentro	www.jobcentro.com/jobcentro/index.asp
IHispano	www.ihispano.com
LatPro	www.latpro.com
National Society of Hispanic MBAs Career Center	www.nshmba.org
SaludosWeb	www.saludos.com
Society of Hispanic Professional Engineers Career Services	www.shpe.org
Spanish JobSite	www.gojobsite.es
TKO International	www.tkointl.com
Zhaopin.com	www.zhaopin.com

Biology/Biotechnology

American Institute of Biological Sciences	www.aibs.org
American Society for Cell Biology	www.ascb.org
American Society of Gene Therapy	www.asgt.org
American Society for Gravitational and Space Biology	www.indstate.edu/asgsb/index.html

Notes
Favorite sites, useful resources

Biology/Biotechnology (continued)

American Society of Limnology and Oceanography	http://aslo.org
American Society for Microbiology	www.asm.org
Bay Area Bioscience Center	www.bayareabioscience.org
BC Biotechnology Alliance [Canada]	www.bcbiotech.ca
Bermuda Biological Station for Research, Inc.	www.bbsr.edu
Biocareer.com	www.biocareer.com
BioExchange.com	www.bioexchange.com
Biofind	www.biofind.com/jobs
BioFlorida	www.bioflorida.com
BioJobNet.com	www.biojobnet.com
BioLinks	www.biolinks.com
Biomedical Engineering Society	www.bmes.org
BioNet Employment Opportunities	www.bio.net/hypermail/EMPLOYMENT/
Bio Research Online	www.bioresearchonline.com
BioSource Technical Service	www.biosource-tech.com
BioSpace Career Center	www.biospace.com/b2/job_index.cfm
BioTech	http://biotech.icmb.utexas.edu/
BioTech Job Site	www.biotechjobsite.com
Biotechnology Association of Alabama	www.bioalabama.com
Biotechnology Association of Maine	www.mainebiotech.org
Biotechnology Calendar, Inc.	www.biotech-calendar.com
Biotechnology Council of New Jersey	www.newjerseybiotech.org
Biotechnology Industry Organization	www.bio.com
	www.biomednet.com
	www.biofind.com
BioView	www.bioview.com
Canadian Society of Biochemistry and Mollecular and Cellular Biologists Experimental Medicine Job Listing	www.medcor.mcgill.ca/DOCS/jobs.html
CanMed [Canada]	www.canmed.com
Cell Press Online	www.cellpress.com
Cen-ChemJobs.org	www.cen-chemjobs.org
Connecticut's BioScience Cluster	www.curenet.org
Drug Information Association Employment Opportunities	www.diahome.org/docs/Jobs/Jobs_index.cfm
HireBio.com	www.hirebio.com
HireHealth.com	www.hirehealth.com
Iowa Biotechnology Association	www.iowabiotech.org
Jobbiology.com	www.jobbiology.com
Jobclinical.com	www.jobclinical.com
Jobgenome.com	www.jobgenome.com
Jobscientist.com	www.jobscientist.com

Notes
Favorite sites, useful resources

Biology/Biotechnology (continued)

Massachusetts Biotechnology Council	www.massbio.org
MdBio, Inc. (Maryland Bioscience)	www.mdbio.org
⛏ Medzilla	www.medzilla.com
MichBIO	www.michbio.org
Nature	www.nature.com
The New York Biotechnology Association	www.nyba.org
North Carolina Biotechnology Center	www.ncbiotech.org
North Carolina Genomics & Bioinformatics Consortium	www.ncgbc.org
Oregon Bioscience Association	www.oregon-bioscience.com
PharmacyWeek.com	www.pharmacyweek.com
RPhrecruiter.com	www.rphrecruiter.com
Rx Career Center	www.rxcareercenter.com
Rx Immigration	www.rximmigration.com
Science Careers	www.sciencecareers.org
Sciencejobs.com	www.sciencejobs.com
SCIENCE Online	www.scienceonline.org
Scijobs.com	www.scijobs.com
SciWeb Biotechnology Career Center	www.biocareer.com/index.cfm
Texas Healthcare & Bioscience Institute	www.thbi.org
Utah Life Sciences Association	www.utahlifescience.com
Virginia Biotechnology Association	www.vabio.org
Washington Biotechnology & Biomedical Association	www.wabio.com
Wisconsin Biotechnology Association	www.wisconsinbiotech.org

Building Industry (see also Construction)

Building Industry Exchange	www.building.org
Builder Online	www.builder.net
EstimatorJobs.com	www.estimatorjobs.com
iHireBuildingTrades.com	www.ihirebuildingtrades.com
MaintenanceEmployment.com	www.maintenanceemployment.com
NewHomeSalesJobs.com	www.newhomesalesjobs.com
ProjectManager.Jobs.com	www.projectmanagerjobs.com
SuperintendentJobs.com	www.superintendentjobs.com
QCEmployMe.com	www.qcemployme.com
Sheet Metal and Air Conditioning Contractor's Association	www.smacna.org

Business

Alley Cat News	www.alleycatnews.com/Index.html
American Society for Quality	http://career-services.asq.org

Notes
Favorite sites, useful resources

Business (continued)

APICS	www.apics.org
Barron's Online	www.barrons.com
Big Charts	www.bigcharts.com
Billboard	www.billboard.com
Biz Journals	www.bizjournals.com
Bloomberg.com	http://about.bloomberg.com/careers/opportunities.html
Business Finance	www.businessfinancemag.com
Business Marketing Association	www.marketing.org
Capital Hill Blue	http://chblue.com
◪ CareerJournal.com	www.careerjournal.com
CareerMarketplace.com	www.careermarketplace.com
Careers In Business	www.careers-in-business.com
CNBC/Career Center	www.cnbc.com
Cnnfn	www.cnnfn.com
CondeNet	www.condenet.com
Corporate Finance Net	www.corpfinet.com
Corporate Watch	www.corpwatch.org
CreditCardJobs.net	www.creditcardjobs.net
Crian's Chicago	www.crainschicagobusiness.com
Customer Service Management	www.csm-us.com
Customer Service University	www.customerserviceuniversity.com
Degree Hunter	www.degreehunter.com
Dow Jones Business Directory	http://businessdirectory.dowjones.com
e-Marketer	www.e-marketer.com
eMoonlighter	www.emoonlighter.com
Entrepreneur	www.entrepreneurmag.com
Fortune	www.fortune.com
Galaxy	www.galaxy.com/galaxy/Business-and-Commerce/Career-and-Employment/
Global Careers	www.globalcareers.com
Harvard Biz Review	www.hbsp.Harvard.edu
Hollywood Reporter	www.hollywoodreporter.com
HomeOfficeJob.com	www.homooffice.com
Hoover's Online	www.hoovers.com
iHireSecurity.com	www.ihiresecurity.com
Inc.	www.inc.com
Industry Week	www.industryweek.com
International Association of Business Communicators	www.iabc.com
International Customer Service Association Job Board	http://secure2.neology.com/ICSA/jobs/employer/welcome.cfm

Notes
Favorite sites, useful resources

WEDDLE's Helping to Maximize Your ROI … Your Return on the Internet

Business (continued)

Internet News	www.internetnews.com
Jane's Defence	www.janes.com
Journal of Commerce	www.joc.com
Kiplinger	www.kiplinger.com
MBAGlobalNet	www.mbaglobalnet.com
MBAJob	www.mbajob.com
MBAmatch.com [England]	www.mbamatch.com
MBA Network	www.mbanetwork.com
MBA Style Magazine	http://members.aol.com/ mbastyle/web/index.html
MedBizPeople.com	www.medbizpeople.com
MeetingJobs.com	www.meetingjobs.com
National Association of Executive Secretaries and Administrative Assistants	www.naesaa.com/verifjb.asp
National Society of Hispanic MBAs Career Center	www.nshmba.org
New York Black MBA	www.nyblackmba.org/ home.shtml
P-Jobs	www.pjobs.org
Pro2Net	www.pro2net.com
Product Development & Management Association	www.pdma.org
ReceptionistJobStore.com	www.receptionistjobstore.com
Red Herring	www.redherring.com
Securities Industry Association Career Resource Center	www.sia.com/career
Smart Money	www.smartmoney.com
Society of Competitive Intelligence Professionals Job Marketplace	www.scip.org/jobs/index.asp
Strategy+Business	www.strategy-business.com
The Street	www.thestreet.com
TANG	www.stern.nyu.edu/~tang
Top Startups	www.topstartups.com
Upside Today	www.upside.com
VAR Business	www.channelweb.com/ sections/careers/jobboard.asp
Vault.com	www.vault.com
WetFeet.com	www.wetfeet.com

-C-

Call Center

CallCenterCareers.com	www.callcentercareers.com
CallCenterJobs.com	www.callcenterjobs.com
Teleplaza	www.teleplaza.com/jp.html

Notes
Favorite sites, useful resources

Career Counseling/Job Search Services

American Evaluation Associaton	www.eval.org/JobBank/jobbank.htm
American Job Search Trainers	www.ajst.org
Association of Career Professionals International	www.iacmp.org
Association of Graduate Careers Advisory Service [United Kingdom]	www.agcas.org.uk
BlueSteps.com	www.bluesteps.com
BrainBench	www.brainbench.com
Canadian Association of Career Educators & Employers	www.cacee.com
CanadianCareers.com	www.canadiancareers.com
CareerFlex.com	www.careerflex.com
CareerHarmony.com	www.careerharmony.com
Career Management International	www.cmi-lmi.com
ComputerPsychologist.com	www.computerpsychologist.com
DDI	http://ddiworld.com
The Engineering Specific Career Advisory Problem-Solving Environment	www.ecn.purdue.edu/escape
ePredix	www.epredix.com
Executive Agent	www.executiveagent.com
ExecutiveResumes.com	www.executiveresumes.com
Exxceed	www.exxceed.com
GetHeadHunted [United Kingdom]	www.getheadhunted.co.uk
Get Me A Job	www.getmeajob.com
GotResumes.com	www.gotresumes.com
JobConnect.org	www.jobconnect.org
National Association of Colleges & Employers	www.jobweb.com
Kaplan Career Services	www.kaplan.com
National Association for College Admission Counseling Career Opportunities	www.nacac.com/classifieds.cfm
National Association of Colleges & Employers (NACE)	www.nacelink.com
National Board for Certified Counselors	www.nbcc.org
National Career Development Association	www.ncda.org
Ready Minds	www.readyminds.com
ResumeBlaster	www.resumeblaster.com
ResumeXPRESS	www.resumexpress.com
Resume-Link	http://resume-link.com
Resume Monkey	www.resumemonkey.com
Resume Network	www.resume-network.com
ResumeRabbit.com	www.resumerabbit.com
Resumes on the Web	www.resweb.com
Resume Workz	www.resumeworkz.com
Skill Scape	www.skillscape.com

Notes
Favorite sites, useful resources

Chemistry

ACS Chemistry.org	www.acs.org
American Association of Brewing Chemists	www.asbcnet.org/SERVICES/career.htm
American Association of Cereal Chemists	www.aaccnet.org/membership/careerplacement.asp
American Association for Clinical Chemistry	www.aacc.org
American Chemical Society cen-chemjobs.org	www.cen-chemjobs.org
American Institute of Chemical Engineers Career Services	www.aiche.org/careers
Chem Jobs	www.chemjobs.net
Chem Web	www.chemweb.com
Chememploy	www.chemploy.com
Chemist Jobs	www.chemistjobs.com
Chemistry & Industry	www.chemind.org/CI/jobs/index.jsp
Chemistry & Industry Magazine	http://pharma.mond.org
iHireChemists.com	www.ihirechemists.com
Intratech	www.intratech1.com
Jobscience Network	www.jobscience.com
Poly Sort	www.polysort.com
Organic Chemistry Jobs Worldwide [Belgium]	www.organicworldwide.net/jobs/jobs.html
Science Careers	www.sciencecareers.org
Sciencejobs.com	www.sciencejobs.com
Scientific American Jobs	www.sciam.com/jobs
Scijobs.org	www.scijobs.org
PlasticsJobsForum.com	www.plasticsjobsforum.com

Child & Elder Care

AuPair In Europe	www.princeent.com/aupair
CareGuide	www.careguide.net
4Nannies.com	www.4nannies.com
SitterByZip	www.sitterbyzip.com/

Classifieds-Newspaper

National

The Wall Street Journal	www.wsj.com
USA Today	www.usatoday.com

Alabama

Birmingham News	www.bhnews.com
Huntsville Times	www.htimes.com

Notes
Favorite sites, useful resources

WEDDLE's Helping to Maximize Your ROI … Your Return on the Internet

Classifieds-Newspaper (continued)

Alabama (continued)
Mobile Register Online							www.mobileregister.com
Montgomery Advertiser						www.montgomeryadvertiser.com
The Tuscaloosa News							www.tuscaloosanews.com

Alaska
Anchorage Daily News							www.alaska.com/akcom/
											  job_network

Fairbanks Daily News							http://fairbanks.abracat.com
Frontiersman									www.frontiersman.com/class
Juneau Empire									www.juneauempire.com
Nome Nugget									www.nomenugget.com

Arizona
Arizona Daily Sun (Flagstaff)					www.azdailysun.com
The Daily Courier (Prescott)					www.prescottaz.com
East Valley Tribune (Mesa)						www.arizonatribune.com
Phoenix News Times								www.phoenixnewstimes.com
Today's News-Herald (Lake Havasu City)			www.havasunews.com

Arkansas
Arkansas Democrat (Little Rock)					www.ardemgaz.com
Benton Courier									www.bentoncourier.com
Jonesboro Sun									www.jonesborosun.com
Ozark Spectator									www.ozarkspectator.com
The Sentinel-Record (Hot Springs)				www.hotsr.com

California
Los Angeles Times								www.latimes.com
Mercury News (San Jose)							www.bayarea.com
Orange County Register							www.ocregister.com
Sacramento Bee									www.sacbee.com
San Francisco Chronicle							www.sfgate.com

Colorado
Aspen Daily News								www.aspendailynews.com
Colorado Springs Independent					www.csindy.com
The Daily Sentinel (Grand Junction)				www.gjsentinel.com
Denver Post										www.denverpost.com
Durango Herald									www.durangoherald.com

Connecticut
The Advocate (Stamford)							www.stamfordadvocate.com
Danbury News-Times								www.newstimes.com
Hartford Courant								www.ctnow.com

Notes
Favorite sites, useful resources

WEDDLE's Helping to Maximize Your ROI ... Your Return on the Internet

Classifieds-Newspaper (continued)

Connecticut (continued)
New Haven Register   www.newhavenregister.com
Waterbury Republican American   wws.rep-am.com

Delaware
Dover Post   www.doverpost.com
The News Journal (Wilmington)   www.delawareonline.com

District of Columbia
The Washington Post   www.washingtonpost.com
Washington Times   www.washtimes.com

Florida
Florida Times Union (Jacksonville)   www.jacksonville.com
Miami Herald   www.miami.com
Orlando Sentinel   www.orlandosentinel.com
Pensacola News Journal   www.pensacolanewstimes.com
St. Petersburg Times   www.sptimes.com

Georgia
The Albany Herald   www.albanyh.surfsouth.com
Atlanta Journal and Constitution   www.accessatlanta.com
Augusta Chronicle   www.augustachronicle.com
Macon Telegraph   www.macon.com
Savannah Morning News   www.savannahnow.com

Hawaii
Hawaii Tribune-Herald (Hilo)   www.hilohawaiitribune.com
Honolulu Advertiser   www.honoluluadvertiser.com
Honolulu Star-Bulletin   www.starbulletin.com
Maui News   www.mauinews.com
West Hawaii Today (Kailua)   www.westhawaiitoday.com

Idaho
Cedar Rapids Gazette   www.gazetteonline.com
The Daily Nonpareil (Council Bluffs)   www.nonpareilonline.com
Des Moines Register   www.dmregister.com
Quad City Times (Davenport)   www.qctimes.com
Sioux City Journal   www.trib.com/scjournal

Illinois
Chicago Tribune   www.chicagotribune.com
Herald & Review (Decatur)   www.herald-review.com
The News-Gazette (Champaigne)   www.news-gazette.com
Register-News (Mount Vernon)   www.register-news.com

Notes
Favorite sites, useful resources

Classifieds-Newspaper (continued)

Illinois (continued)
The State Journal Register (Springfield)   www.sj-r.com

Indiana
The Herald-Times (Bloomington)   www.hoosiertimes.com
Indianapolis Star News   www.indystar.com
The News-Sentinel (Fort Wayne)   www.fortwayne.com
Post-Tribune (Gary)   www.post-trib.com
South Bend Tribune   www.sbinfo.com

Kansas
Daily Union (Junction City)   www.dailyu.com
Kansas City Kansan   www.kansascitykansan.com
Salina Journal   www.saljournal.com
The Topeka Capital Journal   www.cjonline.com
Wichita Eagle   www.kansas.com

Kentucky
The Courier-Journal (Louisville)   www.courier-journal.com
The Daily News (Bowling Green)   www.bgdailynews.com
Grayson County News-Gazette (Leitchfield)   www.gcnewsgazette.com
Lexington Herald Leader   www.kentucky.com
Sentinel News (Shelbyville)   www.shelbyconnect.com

Louisiana
The Advocate (Baton Rouge)   www.advocate.com
The Jackson Independent (Jonesboro)   www.jackson-ind.com
Natchitouches Times   www.natchitouchestimes.com
The Times (Shreveport)   www.shreveporttimes.com
The Times-Picayune (New Orleans)   www.nola.com

Maine
Bangor Daily News   www.bangornews.com
Kennebec Journal (Augusta)   www.kjonline.com
Lewiston Sun Journal   www.sunjournal.com
Portland Press Herald   www.portland.com
The Times Record (Brunswick)   www.timesrecord.com

Maryland
Baltimore Sun   www.sunspot.net
The Capital (Annapolis)   www.hometownannapolis.com
The Herald-Mail (Hagerstown)   www.herald-mail.com
Maryland Times-Press (Ocean City)   www.marylandtimespress.com
The Star Democrat (Easton)   www.stardem.com

Notes
Favorite sites, useful resources

WEDDLE's Helping to Maximize Your ROI ... Your Return on the Internet

Classifieds-Newspaper (continued)

Massachusetts
The Boston Globe   www.boston.com
The Eagle-Tribune (Lawrence)   www.eagletribune.com
The Sun (Lowell)   www.lowellsun.com
The Salem News   www.salemnews.com
Union-News & Sunday Republican (Springfield)   www.masslive.com

Michigan
Ann Arbor News   www.annarbornews.com
Detriot Free Press   www.freep.com
Flint Journal   www.flintjournal.com
Grand Rapids Press   www.gr-press.com
Lansing State Journal   www.lansingstatejournal.com

Minnesota
Duluth News-Tribune   www.duluthsuperior.com
Elk River Star News   www.erstarnews.com
The Journal (New Ulm)   www.oweb.com/NewUlm/journal/home.html
Minneapolis Star Tribune   www.startribune.com
Saint Paul Pioneer Press   www.twincities.com

Mississippi
The Clarion Ledger (Jackson)   www.clarionledger.com
Meridian Star   www.meridianstar.com
The Natchez Democrat   www.natchezdemocrat.com
The Sun Herald (Biloxi)   www.sunherald.com
The Vicksburg Post   www.vicksburgpost.com

Missouri
The Examiner (Independence)   www.examiner.net
Hannibal Courier-Post   www.hannibal.net
Jefferson City News Tribune   www.newstribune.com
Joplin Globe   www.joplinglobe.com
Springfield News-Leader   www.springfieldnews-leader.com

Montana
Billings Gazette   www.billingsgazette.com
Bozeman Daily Chronicle   www.gomontana.com
Helena Independent Record   www.helenair.com
Missoulian   www.missoulian.com
The Montana Standard (Butte)   www.mtstandard.com

Nebraska
Columbus Telegram   www.columbustelegram.com

Notes
Favorite sites, useful resources

WEDDLE's Helping to Maximize Your ROI ... Your Return on the Internet

Classifieds-Newspaper (continued)

Nebraska (continued)
Lincoln Journal Star   www.journalstar.com
North Platte Telegraph   www.nptelegraph.com
Omaha World-Herald   www.omaha.com
Scotts Bluff Star-Herald   www.starherald.com

Nevada
Elko Daily Free Press   www.elkodaily.com
Las Vegas Review-Journal   www.lvrj.com
Las Vegas Sun   www.lasvegassun.com
Nevada Appeal (Carson City)   www.nevadaappeal.com
Reno Gazette Journal   www.rgj.com

New Hampshire
Concord Monitor   www.concordmonitor.com
Keene Sentinel   www.keenesentinel.com
Portsmouth Herald   www.seacoastonline.com
The Telegraph (Nashua)   www.nashuatelegraph.com
The Union Leader (Manchester)   www.theunionleader.com

New Jersey
Asbury Park Press   www.app.com
Courier-Post (Cherry Hill)   www.courierpostonline.com
The Montclair Times   www.montclairtimes.com
The Star Ledger (Newark)   www.nj.com
The Trentonian   www.trentonian.com

New Mexico
Albuquerque Journal   www.abqjournal.com
The Gallup Independent   www.gallupindependent.com
Los Alamos Monitor   www.lamonitor.com
Santa Fe New Mexican   www.sfnewmexican.com
The Silver City Daily Press   www.thedailypress.com

New York
Albany Democrat Herald   www.dhonline.com
Ithaca Times   www.ithacatimes.com
New York Post   www.nypost.com
The New York Times   www.nytimes.com
Syracuse New Times   www.newtimes.com

North Carolina
Charlotte Observer   www.charlotte.com
Greensboro News-Record   www.news-record.com
News & Observer (Raleigh)   www.newsobserver.com

Notes
Favorite sites, useful resources

WEDDLE's Helping to Maximize Your ROI ... Your Return on the Internet

Classifieds-Newspaper (continued)

North Carolina (continued)
Wilmington Star					www.wilmingtonstar.com
Winston-Salem Journal				www.journalnow.com

North Dakota
Bismarck Tribune				www.bismarcktribune.com
Grand Forks Herald				www.grandforks.com
The Jamestown Sun				www.jamestownsun.com
Minot Daily News				www.minotdailynews.com

Ohio
Cincinnati Enquirer				www.enquirer.com
The Cleveland Nation				www.clnation.com
Columbus Dispatch				www.dispatch.com
Dayton Daily News				www.daytondailynews.com
Springfield News Sun				www.springfieldnewssun.com

Oklahoma
Altus Times					www.altustimes.com
Lawton Constitution				www.lawton-constitution.com
The Oklahoman (Oklahoma City)			www.newsok.com
Ponca City News					www.poncacitynews.com
Tulsa World					www.tulsaworld.com

Oregon
East Oregonian (Pendleton)			www.eonow.com
The Oregonian (Portland)			www.oregonian.com
The Register-Guard (Eugene)			www.registerguard.com
Springfield News				www.hometownnews.com
Statesman Journal (Salem)			www.statesmanjournal.copm

Pennsylvania
Erie Daily Times-News				www.goerie.com
The Philadelphia Inquirer			www.philly.com
Plttsburg Post-Gazette				www.post-gazette.com
Scranton Times Tribune				www.scrantontimes.com
Tho Timos Loader (Willkcs Barrc)		www.timesleader.com

Rhode Island
The Narragansett Times (Wakefield)		www.narragansetttimes.com
The Pawtucket Times				www.pawtuckettimes.com
Providence Journal Bulletin			www.projo.com
Sakonnet Times (Portsmouth)			www.eastbayri.com

Find Great Talent. ← WEDDLE's 2004 Recruiter's Guide

Notes
Favorite sites, useful resources

WEDDLE's Helping to Maximize Your ROI ... Your Return on the Internet

Classifieds-Newspaper (continued)

South Carolina
Camden Chronicle Independent — www.chronicle-independent.com
Free Times (Columbia) — www.free-times.com
The Greenville News — www.greenvilleonline.com
The Post and Courier (Charleston) — www.charleston.net
The Sun Times (Myrtle Beach) — www.myrtlebeachonline.com

South Dakota
Argus Leader (Sioux Falls) — www.argusleader.com
Brookings Daily Register — www.brookingsregister.com
The Capital Journal (Pierre) — www.capjournal.com
The Freeman Courier — www.freemansd.com
Huron Plainsman — www.plainsman.com

Tennessee
Chattanooga Times Free Press — www.timesfreepress.com
Daily Post-Athenian — www.dpa.xtn.net
Knoxville News Sentinel — www.knoxnews.com
Memphis Flyer — www.memphisflyer
The Tennessean (Nashville) — www.onnashville.com

Texas
Austin American-Statesman — www.austin360.com
Dallas Morning News — www.dallasnews.com
El Paso Times — www.elpasotimes.com
Houston Chronicle — www.chron.com
San Antonio Express News — www.mysanantonio.com

Utah
The Daily Herald (Provo) — www.harktheherald.com
Herald Journal (Logan) — www.hjnews.com
Salt Lake Tribune — www.sltrib.com
Standard-Examiner (Ogden) — www.standard.net

Vermont
Addison County Independent (Middlebury) — www.addisonindependent.com
Burlington Free Press — www.burlingtonfreepress.com
Deerfield Valley News (West Dover) — www.dvalnews.com
Stowe Reporter — www.stowereporter.com
Valley News (White River Junction) — www.vnews.com

Virginia
The Daily Progress (Charlottesville) — www.dailyprogress.com
Danville Register Bee — www.registerbee.com
The News-Advance (Lynchburg) — www.newsadvance.com

Notes
Favorite sites, useful resources

WEDDLE's Helping to Maximize Your ROI ... Your Return on the Internet

Classifieds-Newspaper (continued)

Virginia (continued)
Richmond Times-Dispatch					www.timesdispatch.com
Virginian-Pilot (Norfolk)					www.pilotonline.com

Washington
The Columbian (Vancouver)					www.columbian.com
The News Tribune (Tacoma)					www.tribnet.com
The Olympian (Olympia)					www.theolympian.com
Seattle Post-Intelligencer					www.seattlepi.nwsource.com
The Spokesman-Review (Spokane)				www.spokane.net

West Virginia
Charlestown Daily Mail					www.www.dailymail.com
Clarksburg Exponent Telegram					www.cpubco.com
The Dominion Post (Morgantown)				www.dominionpost.com
Times West Virginian (Fairmont)				www.timeswv.com
Wheeling News-Register					www.news-register.com

Wisconsin
Green Bay Press Gazette					www.greenbaypressgazette.com
The Journal Times (Racine)					www.journaltimes.com
La Crosse Tribune						www.lacrossetribune.com
Milwaukee Journal Sentinel					www.jsonline.com
Wisconsin State Journal (Madison)				www.madison.com

Wyoming
Douglas Budget						www.douglas-budget.com
Wyoming Tribune-Eagle					www.wyomingnews.com

College/Internships/Entry Level/Graduate School Graduates

General
Aboutjobs.com						www.aboutjobs.com
Adguide's Employment Web Site					www.adguide.com
AfterCollege.com						www.aftercollege.com
Around Campus						www.aroundcampus.com
THE BLACK COLLEGIAN Online					www.blackcollegian.com
Campus Career Center					www.campuscareercenter.com
Canadian Association of Career Educators
 & Employers						www.cacee.com
Career Chase						www.careerchase.net
Career Conferences						www.careerconferences.com
Career Connections						www.resumeexpert.com
Career Explorer						http://cx.bridges.com
Careerfair.com						www.careerfair.com

Notes
Favorite sites, useful resources

College/Internships/Entry Level/Graduate School Graduates (con't)

College Central Network	www.collegecentral.com
College Club	www.collegeclub.com
CollegeGrad.com	www.collegegrad.com
College Job Board	www.collegejobboard.com
CollegeJournal.com	www.collegejournal.com
College News Online	www.collegenews.com/home_shop.asp
College PowerPrep	www.powerprep.com
CollegeRecruiter.com	www.collegerecruiter.com
Colleges	www.colleges.com
eCampusRecruiter.com	www.ecampusrecruiter.com
EntryLevelJobs.net	www.entryleveljobs.net
Experience	www.experience.com
Graduating Engineer Online	www.graduateengineer.com
Graduating Engineer & Computer Careers Online	www.careertech.com
Gradunet [United Kingdom]	www.gradunet.co.uk
InternJobs.com	www.internjobs.com
Internship Programs	www.internshipprograms.com
Internships	www.internships.com
Internweb	www.internweb.com
Job Gusher	www.jobgusher.com
job-hunt.org	www.job-hunt.org
JobPostings.net	www.jobpostings.net
Mapping Your Future	www.mapping-your-future.org
MBAGlobalNet	www.mbaglobalnet.com
MBA Job	www.mbajob.com
MBAmatch.com [England]	www.mbamatch.com
MBA Network [Canada]	www.mbanetwork.ca
MBA Style Magazine	http://members.aol.com/mbastyle/web/index.html
Monster Campus	http://campus.monster.com/
National Association of Colleges & Employers (NACE)	www.nacelink.com
National Society of Collegiate Scholars Career Connection	www.nscs.org/CareerConnections/index.cfm
National Society of Hispanic MBAs Career Center	www.nshmba.org
New York Black MBA	www.nyblackmba.org/
OverseasJobs.com	www.overseasjobs.com
Paid Internships	www.paidinternships.com
Peterson's	www.petersons.com
Princeton Review Online	www.review.com/career/Career_homepage.html
Prospects Web [United Kingdom]	http://buzzard.csu.man.ac.uk
Reference Now	www.referencenow.com
ResortJobs.com	www.resortjobs.com

Notes
Favorite sites, useful resources

WEDDLE's Helping to Maximize Your ROI ... Your Return on the Internet

College/Internships/Entry Level/Graduate School Graduates (con't)

SallieMae	www.truecareers.com
Snag A Job	www.snagajob.com
Stanford Linear Accelerator Center	www.slac.stanford.edu
Student Advantage	www.studentadvantage.com
Student Affairs	www.studentaffairs.com
Student Awards	www.studentawards.com
Student Planet	www.studentplanet.com
Study Abroad	www.studyabroad.com
SummerJobs.com	www.summerjobs.com
Super College	www.supercollege.com
Teens 4 Hire	www.teens4hire.org
University Links	www.ulinks.com
US Interns	www.usinterns.com
Virtual Edge	www.virtual-edge.net
Virtual Intern	www.virtualintern.com
Youth@Work	www.youthatwork.org

College/University Affiliated

California State University - Chico	www.csuchico.edu/plc/jobs.html
Career Development Center at Rensselier Polytechnic Institute	www.cdc.rpi.edu
Case Western Reserve University	www.cwru.edu
The Catholic University of America Career Services Office	http://careers.cua.edu/studalum/progserv.htm
Clemson University	www.clemson.edu
Cornell Career Services	http://student-jobs.ses.cornell.edu
Drake University	www.drake.edu
Drexel University	www.drexel.edu/scdc/
Duke University Job Resources	http://career.studentaffairs.duke.edu
Emory University Rollins School of Public Health	www.sph.emory.edu/studentservice
Foothill-De Anza Community College	www.foothill.fhda.edu
Georgia State University Career Services	www.gsu.edu/dept/admin/plc/homepage4.html
Georgia Tech Career Services Office	www.career.gatech.edu
Loyola College	www.lattanze.loyola.edu
Nova Southeastern University	www.nova.edu
Oakland University	www2.oakland.edu/careerservices
Purdue University Management Placement Office	www.mgmt.purdue.edu/departments/gcs/
San Francisco State University Instructional Technologies	www.itec.sfsu.edu
University of Arkansas	www.uark.edu
U.C. Berkeley Work-Study Programs	http://workstudy.berkeley.edu

Notes
Favorite sites, useful resources

WEDDLE's Helping to Maximize Your ROI ... Your Return on the Internet

College/Internships/Entry Level/Graduate School Graduates (con't)
College/University Affiliated (continued)

University of Virginia Career Planning and Placement	www.virginia.edu/~career
University of Wisconsin-Madison School of Business Career Center	www.bus.wisc.edu/career/default1.asp
Washington and Lee University	http://netlink.wlu.edu
Worcester Polytechnic Institute	www.wpi.edu

Computer
(See High Tech/Technical/Technology and Information Technology/Information Systems)

Computer-Aided Design, Manufacturing & Engineering

American Design Drafting Association	www.adda.org
Auto CAD Job Network	www.acjn.com
CAD Job Mart	www.cadjobmart.com
Computer-Aided Three-Dimensional Interactive Application Job Network	www.catjn.com
e-Architect	www.e-architect.com
IDEAS Job Network	www.ideasjn.com
Just CAD Jobs	www.justCADjobs.com
Manufacturing Jobs	www.mfgjbs.com
Manufacturing.Net	www.manufacturing.net
Pro/E Job Network	www.pejn.com
UG Job Network (Unigraphics)	www.ugjn.com

Construction (see also Engineering)

A/E/C JobBank	www.aecjobbank.com
Bconstructive [United Kingdom]	www.bconstructive.co.uk
Builder Online	www.builder.hw.net
Building.com	www.building.com
Careers In Construction	www.careersinconstruction.com
CarpenterJobs.com	www.carpenterjobs.com
Construction/Careers	www.construction.com
ConstructionEducation.com	www.constructioneducation.com
Construction Gigs	www.constructiongigs.com
ConstructionJobs.com	www.constructionjobs.com
ConstructionOnly.com	www.constructiononly.com
Electrical Employment	www.cossin.com/page3.html
Engineering News Record	www.enr.com
Environmental Construction Engineering Architectural Jobs Online	www.eceajobs.com
Estimator Jobs	www.estimatorjobs.com
iHireBuildingTrades.com	www.ihirebuildingtrades.com

Notes
Favorite sites, useful resources

Construction (continued)

iHireConstruction.com — www.ihireconstruction.com
Jobsite.com — www.jobsite.com
Maintenance Engineer — www.maintenanceemployment.com
Materials Jobs — www.welding-engineer.com
MEPatwork.com [mechanical, electrical, plumbing] — www.mepatwork.com
Metal Working Portal — http://metal-working.tradeworlds.com
National Association of Women in Construction — www.nawic.org
Painting and Coatings — www.paintandcoatings.com
Plumbing Careers — www.plumbingcareers.com
PLUMBjob.com — www.plumbjob.com
ProjectManagerJobs.com — www.projectmanagerjobs.com
QCEmployMe.com — www.qcemployme.com
Right of Way — www.rightofway.com
SuperintendentJobs.com — www.superintendentjobs.com
Trade Jobs Online — http://trades.buildfind.com
TradesJobs.com — www.tradesjobs.com
Trade Jobs Online — www.tradejobsonline.com
HVAC Mall — www.hvacmall.com
Welding Jobs — www.weldingjobs.com

Consultants

Career Lab — www.careerlab.com
★ Computerwork.com — www.computerwork.com
ConsultLink.com — www.consultlink.com
Independent Human Resource Consultants Association — www.ihrca.com/Contract_Regular.asp
The Independent Consultants Network — www.inconet.com
Medical Consultants Network — www.mcn.com

Contract Employment/Part Time Employment (see also Search Firms)

Ants — www.ants.com
Bookatemp.co.uk [United Kingdom] — www.bookatemp.co.uk
Camp Jobs — www.campjobs.com
Camp Staff — www.campstaff.com
Contract Employment Weekly Jobs Online — www.ceweekly.com
Contract Engineering.com — www.contractengineering.com
Contract Job Hunter — www.cjhunter.com
Contracts247 [United Kingdom] — www.contracts247.co.uk
Creative Freelancers — www.freelancers.com
DoAAProject.com — www.doaproject.com
eMoonlighter — www.emoonlighter.com
ExperienceNet.com — www.experiencenet.com
ForContractRecruiters.com — www.forcontractrecruiters.com

Notes
Favorite sites, useful resources

WEDDLE's Helping to Maximize Your ROI ... Your Return on the Internet

Contract Employment/Part Time Employment (continued)

FreeAgent.com	www.freeagent.com/Myhome.asp
Free Agent Nation	www.freeagentnation.com
Freelance Work X	www.freelanceworkexchange.com
Freelancers/TalentX	www.talentx.com
Guru.com	www.guru.com
Hands on Solutions [United Kingdom]	www.handsonsolutions.com
Homeworkers	www.homeworkers.com
Jobs in Logistics	www.jobsinlogistics.com
Labor Ready	www.laborready.com
LifeguardingJobs.com	www.lifeguardingjobs.com
Mediabistro	www.mediabistro.com
★ Net-Temps.com	www.net-temps.com
Roadwhore	www.roadwhore.com
Sheet Metal and Air Conditioning Contractor's Association	www.smacna.org
Snag A Job	www.snagajob.com
Sologig	www.sologig.com
Subcontract.com	www.subcontract.com
Summer Jobs	www.summerjobs.com
TelecommutingJobs	www.tjobs.com
Temps Online.co.uk [United Kingdom]	www.tempsonline.co.uk
Tempz	www.tempz.com
U Bid Contract Contracting Portal	www.ubidcontract.com

Culinary/Food Preparation (see also Hospitality)

American Association of Brewing Chemists	www.scisoc.org
American Association of Cereal Chemists	www.scisoc.org
American Culinary Federation	www.acfchefs.org
Bakery-Net	www.bakerynet.com
Careers in Food	www.careersinfood.com
Chef Jobs Network	http://chefjobsnetwork.com
Escoffier Online	www.escoffier.com
Food And Drink Jobs.com	www.foodanddrinkjobs.com
Food Industry Jobs	www.foodindustryjobs.com
iHireChefs.com	www.ihirechefs.com
Restaurant Careers	www.restaurant-careers.com
Restaurant Jobs	www.restaurantjobs.com
Star Chefs	www.starchefs.com

**Looking for a new or better job?   Looking for top talent?
Use WEDDLE's publications. See the Catalog in this book.**

Notes
Favorite sites, useful resources

-D-

Data Processing

Black Data Processing Association Online — www.bdpa.org
Database Analyst — www.databaseanalyst.com

Dental

American Dental Hygienists' Association — www.adha.org/careerinfo/index.html
California Dental Hygienists' Association Employment Opportunities — www.cdha.org/advertising/adpage.html
DentalJobs.com — www.dentaljobs.com
Foothill College Dental Hygiene Job Board — www.foothill.fhda.edu/bio/programs/dentalh/jobs.cgi?view_entries
iHireDental.com — www.ihiredental.com
JobDental.com — www.jobdental.com
JobDentist.com — www.jobdentist.com
JobDentistry.com — www.jobdentistry.com
JobHygienist.com — www.jobhygienist.com
MedHunters Dental Hygiene — www.medhunters.com/jobs/Dent_Hyg.html
OverseasDentist.com — www.overseasdentist.com
SmileJobs.com — www.smilejobs.com

Diversity

Able to Work — www.abletowork.org
The Ada Project — www.cs.yale.edu/HTML/YALE/CS/HyPlans/tap/tap.html
AdvancingWomen.net — www.advancingwomen.net
Afro-Americ@ — www.afro.com
Alianza (Latino) — www.alianza.org
American Society of Women Accountants Employment Opportunities — www.aswa.org/wanted.html
Asia-Net — www.asia-net.com
AsianAvenue.com — www.asianavenue.com
Association of Latino Professionals in Finance & Accounting Job Postings — www.alpfa.org/professi/careoppo.asp
Association for Women in Communications — www.womcom.org
Association for Women in Computing — www.awc-hq.org
Best Diversity Employers — www.bestdiversityemployers.com
Bilingual-Jobs — www.bilingual-jobs.com
Black Career Women Online — www.bcw.org
THE BLACK COLLEGIAN Online — www.blackcollegian.com

WEDDLE's Helping to Maximize Your ROI ... Your Return on the Internet

Notes
Favorite sites, useful resources

Diversity (continued)

Black Data Processing Association Online	www.bpda.org
Black E.O.E. Journal	www.blackeoejournal.com/jobsearch.html
Black Enterprise Magazine Career Center	www.blackenterprise.com
Blackgeeks	www.blackgeeks.com
BlackPlanet.com	www.blackplanet.com
Black Voices	www.blackvoices.com
Black World	www.blackworld.com
The Black World Today	http://tbwt.com
Canada's Fifty-Plus	www.fifty-plus.net
Career Moves	www.jvsjobs.org
Career Women	www.careerwomen.com
Chicago Chinese Computing Professional Assn	www.cccpa.org
Choice Employment	www.choiceemployment.com/
Christian Jobs Online	www.christianjobs.com
CLNET (Chicano/Latino Communities)	http://latino.sscnet.ucla.edu
Commission on Aging	www.ncoa.org
Corporate Diversity Search	www.corpdiversitysearch.com
Disability Job Site	www.disabilityjobsite.com
Diversity Careers	www.diversitycareers.com
Diversity Central	www.diversityhotwire.com
Diversity Employment	www.diversityemployment.com
Diversity Events	www.diversityevents.com
DiversityInc.com	www.diversityinc.com
Diversity Job Network	www.diversityjobnetwork.com
DiversityLink	www.diversitylink.com
Diversity Search	www.diversitysearch.com
El Nuevo Herald	www.elherald.com
Electra	http://electra.com
Equal Opportunity Publications, Inc.	www.eop.com
Ethnicity	www.ethnicity.com
Feminist Career Center	www.feminist.org/911/911jobs.html
Fifty On [United Kingdom]	www.fiftyon.co.uk/frameset.asp
Fifty Something Jobs	www.fiftysomethingjobs.com
Financial Women International Careers	www.fwi.org/careers/career.htm
Forty Plus	http://web.sirius.com/~40plus/#contact
Galaxy	http://galaxy.einet.net/galaxy.html
GayWork.com	www.gaywork.com
GetaMom.com	www.getamom.com
HierosGamos	www.hg.org
Hire Diversity	www.hirediversity.com
Hispanic Business.com	www.hispanicbusiness.com/
Hispanic Online	www.hispaniconline.com

Notes
Favorite sites, useful resources

Diversity (continued)

I Can Online	www.icanonline.net
iHispano.com	www.ihispano.com
IMDiversity.com	www.imdiversity.com
Recruit International Career Information, Inc.	www.rici.com
Jewish Vocational Service Jobs Page	www.jvsjobs.org
Job Ability	www.jobability.com
Job Access	www.jobaccess.com
Job Accommodation Network	http://janweb.icdi.wvu.edu
Jobs 4 Women	http://jobs4women.com
Job Latino	www.joblatino.com
Laborum.com	www.laborum.com
LatinoWeb	www.latinoweb.com
LatPro	www.latpro.com
Lifeprint	www.lifeprint.org
MiContacto	www.micontacto.com
MiGente.com	www.migente.com
Minorities Job Bank	www.iminorities.com
Minority Career Network	www.minoritycareernet.com
MinorityNurse.com	www.minoritynurse.com
Minority Professional Network	www.minorityprofessionalnetwork.com
Mo Better Jobs	www.mobetterjobs.com
The Multicultural Advantage	www.tmaonline.net
National Association of Hispanic Nurses Houston Chapter	www.nahnhouston.org
National Association of African Americans in Human Resources	www.naaahr.org
National Association of Black Accountants, Inc. Career Center	www.nabainc.jobcontrolcenter.com
National Association of Women in Construction	www.nawic.org
National Black MBA Association, Inc.	www.nbmbaa.org
National Black MBA Association New York Chapter	www.nyblackmba.org
National Diversity Newspaper Job Bank	www.newsjobs.com
National Femal Executives	www.nafe.com
Hispanic Chamber of Commerce JobCentro	www.jobcentro.com/jobcentro/index.asp
National Network of Commercial Real Estate Women Job Bank	www.nncrew.org/job_bank/job_bank_introduction_frm.html
National Organization for Professional Advancement of Black Chemists and Chemical Engineers University of Michigan Chapter	www.engin.umich.edu/soc/nobcche
National Society of Black Engineers	www.nsbe.org

Notes
Favorite sites, useful resources

Diversity (continued)

National Society of Hispanic MBAs Career Center	www.nshmba.org
National Urban League	www.nul.org
NBDC	www.business-disability.com
NetNoir	www.netnoir.com
New Mobility	www.newmobility.com
Pride Source	www.pridesource.com
ProFound.com	www.profound.com
RetiredBrains	www.retiredbrains.com
Saludos Web Site	www.saludos.com
Sistahspace	www.sistahspace.com
Society of Hispanic Professional Engineers Career Services	www.shpe.org
Society for Human Resource Management Diversity Page	www.shrm.org/hrlinks/div.htm
Society of Women Engineers Career Services	www.societyofwomenengineers.org/specialservices/careerservices.aspx
US Empleos	www.usempleos.com
Vets of Color	www.vetsofcolor.com
VISA Jobs	www.h1visajobs.com/
Webgrrls International	www.webgrrls.com
Women.com	www.women.com
Women Connect.com	www.womenconnect.com
Women In Communications Washington, D.C. Chapter	www.awic-dc.org
Women in Technology	www.worldWIT.org
Women in Technology International (WITI) 4Hire	www.witi4hire.com
Women's Executive Network	www.thewen.com
Women's Finance Exchange	www.t-i-a.com/networks/wfe.html
Women's Wear Daily	www.wwd.com
Womens-work	www.womans-work.com

-E-

Economists

American Agricultural Economics Association	www.aaes.org
E-JOE: European Job Opportunites for Economists	http://rfe.org/JobGrant/E-JEurJobOpe.html
Inomics	www.inomics.com
JobSlide.com	http://jobslide.com/directory/FinanceIns/Economist/
JOE: Job Opportunities for Economists	http://www.eco.utexas.edu/joe/

Notes
Favorite sites, useful resources

Education/Academia

About.com	http://jobsearch.mining.co.com/msubteach.htm
Academe This Week	www.chronicle.com
Academia [Australia]	http://academia.anu.edu.au/New
Academic Employment Network	www.academploy.com
Academic Physician & Scientist	www.acphysci.com
Academic Position Network	www.apnjobs.com
American Agricultural Economic Association Employment Service	www.aaea.org/classifieds
American Educational Research Association Job Openings	www.aera.net/jobposts/
American Institute of Physics Career Services	www.aip.org/industry.html
American Psychological Society Observer Job Listings	www.psychologicalscience.org/jobs
ArtJob Online	www.artjob.com
Association of Graduate Careers Advisory Service [United Kingdom]	www.agcas.org.uk
The Association for Institutional Research	www.airweb.org/page.asp?page=2
Association of Teachers of Technical Writing	http://english.ttu.edu/attwtest/default.asp
ATeacherJobSearch.com	www.ateacherjobsearch.com
Canadian Society of Biochemistry and Mollecular and Cellular Biologists Experimental Medicine Job Listing	www.medcor.mcgill.ca/EXPMED/DOCS/jobs.html
CCJobsOnline.com	www.ccjobsonline.com
The Chronicle of Higher Education Academe This Week	http://chronicle.merit.edu/jobs
Coach's Nationwide Job Board	www.coachhelp.com/jobs.htm
College and University Personnel Association JobLine	www.cupa.org/jobline/jobline.htm
Community Learning Network	www.cln.org
Computing Research Association Job Announcements	www.cra.org/jobs/main/cra_jobs.html
Council for Advancement & Support of Education Jobs Online	www.case.org/jobs
Dave's ESL Café	www.eslcafe.com
The Directory Recruitment Service [Australia]	www.thedirectory.aone.net.au/page8.htm
e-Math	www.ams.org
Education Week on the Web	www.edweek.org
Education World Jobs	www.education-world.com/jobs
EducatorJob.com	www.educatorjob.com
EFLWEB: English as a Second or Foreign Language	www.u-net.com/eflweb/contents.htm

Notes
Favorite sites, useful resources

Education/Academia (continued)

The ESL Café's Job Center	www.pacificnet.net/~sperling/jobcenter.html
ESL Worldwide	www.eslworldwide.com
Foothill-De Anza Community College District	www.fhda.edu/district/hr/employment.html
GeoWeb Jobs	www.ggrweb.com
GreatInfo.com	www.greatinfo.com/business_cntr/career.html
Hire-Ed	www.hireed.net
HigherEdJobs.com	www.higheredjobs.com
History of Science Society	www.depts.washington.edu/hssexec
Hudson Institute	www.hudson.org
Independent School Management	www.isminc.com/mm.html
International Academic Job Market [Australia]	www.camrev.com.au/sharejobs.html
Jaeger's Ince-Math	www.ams.org/employment
JOE: Job Opportunities for Economists	www.eco.utexas.edu/joe
Jobs in Higher Education Geographical Listings	http://volvo.gslis.utexas.edu/~acadres/jobs/index.html
Jobs in Linguistics	www.linguistlist.org/jobsindex.html
Jobs.ac.uk [United Kingdom]	www.jobs.ac.uk
K-12 Jobs	www.k12jobs.com
Math-Jobs	www.math-jobs.com
The Minerals, Metals, Materials Scoiety JOM	www.tms.org/pubs/journals/JOM/classifieds.html
MinorityNurse.com	www.minoritynurse.com
Music Library Association Job Placement	www.music.indiana.edu/Som/placement/index.html
NationJob Network-Education Job Openings	www.nationjob.com/education
National Association for College Admission Counseling Career Opportunities	www.nacac.com/classifieds.cfm
National Council of Teachers of Math Jobs	www.nctm.org
National Information Services and Systems [United Kingdom]	www.nlss.ac.uk/cr/index.htm/#nb
National Teacher Recruitment	www.recruitingteachers.com
Now Hiring Teachers	www.nowhiringteachers.com
PhDjobs.com	www.phdjobs.com
Phds.org	http://phds.org
PLATO	www.skillsnet.com
The Private School Employment Network	www.privateschooljobs.com
Education Placement and Career Services	http://careers.soemadison.wisc.edu

Notes
Favorite sites, useful resources

Education/Academia (continued)

School Staff	www.schoolstaff.com
Superintendent Jobs	www.superintendentjobs.com
Teacher Jobs	www.teacherjobs.com
Teachers of English to Speakers of Other Languages Job Finder	www.tesol.org
THESIS: The Times Higher Education Supplement InterView Service [United Kingdom]	www.thesis.co.uk
University of Illinois at Urbana-Champaign Grad School of Library & Information Science Placement Online-Library Job Service	http://carousel.lis.uiuc.edu/

Engineering

A1A Jobs	www.a1ajobs.com
A/E/C Job Bank	www.aecjobbank.com
AeroJobs	www.aerojobs.com
Aeroindustryjobs	www.aeroindustryjobs.com
Alpha Systems	www.jobbs.com
American Chemical Society cen-chemjobs.org	www.cen-chemjobs.org
American Institute of Chemical Engineers Career Services	www.aiche.org/careers
American Jobs.com	www.americanjobs.com
American Society of Agricultural Engineering	www.asae.org/membership/career.html
American Society of Civil Engineers	www.asce.org
American Society of Mechanical Engineers Career Center	www.asme.org/jobs
Biomedical Engineering Society	www.bmes.org
CadJobMart	www.cadjobmart.com
Career Center @ Semiconductor Online	www.semiconductoronline.com
Career Marketplace Network	www.careermarketplace.com
CED Magazine	www.cedmagazine.com
CFD Online (Computational Fluid Dynamics)	www.cfd-online.com
Chemical Engineer	www.chemicalengineer.com
Civil Engineering Jobs	www.civilengineeringjobs.com
CIVILjobs.com	www.civiljobs.com
Contract Employment Weekly	www.ceweekly.com
Contract Engineering.com	www.contractengineering.com
Computer-Aided Three-Dimensional Interactive Application Job Network	www.catjn.com
Degree Hunter	www.degreehunter.com
Discover Jobs	www.discoverjobs.com
Drilling Research Institute Classifieds	www.drillers.com/classifieds.cfm

Notes
Favorite sites, useful resources

Engineering (continued)

EG3.com	www.eg3.com
EDN Access	www.ednmag.com
EE Times	www.eet.com
Electric Job.com	www.electricjob.com
Electric Net	www.electricnet.com
Electrical Engineer	www.electricalengineer.com
Electronic News Online	www.electronicnews.com
EngineerJobs.com	www.engineerjobs.com
Engineering Central	www.engcen.com/jobbank.htm
Engineering Classifieds	www.engineeringclassifieds.com
Engineering Giant	www.engineergiant.com
Engineering Institute of Canada	www.eic-ici.ca
Engineering Job Source	www.engineerjobs.com
EngineeringJobs.com	www.engineeringjobs.com
Engineering News Record	www.enr.com
Engineer Web	www.engineerweb.com
The Engineering Specific Career Advisory Problem-Solving Environment	www.ecn.purdue.edu/escape
The Engineering Technology Site [United Kingdom]	www.engineers4engineers.co.uk
Environmental Construction Engineering Architectural Jobs Online	www.eceajobs.com
GeoWeb Jobs	www.ggrweb.com
Graduating Engineer Online	www.graduatingengineer.com
Graduating Engineer & Computer Careers Online	www.careertech.com
Humanys.com	www.humanys.com
iCivil Engineer	www.icivilengineer.com/jobs
IDEAS Job Network	www.ideasjn.com
iHireEngineering.com	www.ihireengineering.com
iHireManufacturingEngineers.com	www.ihiremanufacturing engineers.com
Industrial Engineer	www.industrialengineer.com
Institute of Electrical & Electronics Engineers Job Site	www.ieee.org/jobs
The Instrumentation, Systems and Automation Society Online ISA Jobs	www.isa.org/isa_es
Job Net	www.jobnet.org
Job Oil	www.joboil.com
Job Search for Engineers	www.interec.net
Jobs 4 Engineers	www.ajob4engineers.com
Jobs for Mechanical Engineers	www.mechanicalengineer.com
The Mechanic	www.the-mechanic.com/jobs.html
Mechanical Engineers Magazine Online	www.memagazine.org
The Minerals, Metals, Materials Society JOM	www.tms.org/pubs/journals/JOM/classifieds.html
National Association of Grad & Prof Students	www.nagps.org

WEDDLE's Helping to Maximize Your ROI ... Your Return on the Internet

Notes
Favorite sites, useful resources

www.WEDDLES.com

Engineering (continued)

National Association of Radio and Telecommunications Engineers	www.narte.org
National Electrical Contractors Association	www.necanet.org
National Organization for Professional Advancement of Black Chemists and Chemical Engineers University of Michigan Chapter	www.engin.umich.edu/ soc/nobcche
National Society of Black Engineers	www.nsbe.org
National Society of Professional Engineers Employment	www.nspe.org/ em-home.asp
National Technical Services Association	www.ntsa.com
National Society of Black Engineers	www.nsbe.org
NukeWorker.com	www.nukeworker.com
Oil & Gas Jobs	www.earthworks-jobs.com/comm.htm
Oil Career	www.oilcareer.com
Oil Industry Jobs	www.oilsurvey.com
Oil Job	www.oiljob.com
Plastic Pro	www.plasticpro.com
Plastics Jobs Forum.com	www.plasticsjobsforum.com
PlumbingCareers.com	www.plumbingcareers.com
PLUMBjob.com	www.plumbjob.com
Power Magazine	www.powermag.com
Product Design and Development Online Career Center	www.manufacturing.nt/dn
Pro/E Job Network	www.pejn.com
RF Globalnet	www.rfglobalnet.com
Right Of Way	www.rightofway.com
Roadwhore	www.roadwhore.com
Semi Web	www.semiweb.com/employment
Society of Automotive Engineers Job Board	www.sae.org/careers/recrutad.htm
Society of Hispanic Professional Engineers Career Services	www.shpe.org
Society for Information Display	http://www.sid.org/jobmart/jobmart.html
Society of Women Engineers Career Services	www.societyofwomenengineers.org/specialservices/careerservices.aspx
Space Jobs	www.spacejobs.com
SPIE Web-International Society for Optical Engineering	www.spieworks.com
Systems Engineer	www.systemsengineer.com
Tech Employment	www.techemployment.com
Test & Measurement World	www.tmworld.com

Notes
Favorite sites, useful resources

Engineering (continued)

UG Job Network (Unigraphics CAD/CAM/CAE)	www.ugjn.com
Questlink.com	www.questlink.com
Wireless Design Online	www.wirelessdesignonline.com
Worldwide Worker	www.worldwideworker.com

Entertainment/Acting

101 Hollywood Boulevard	http:members.aol.com/crewjobs/index.htm
4 Entertainment Jobs	www.4entertainmentjobs.com
Airwaves Media Web	www.airwaves.com
Airwaves Media Web	www.airwaves.com
Answers4Dancers.com	www.answers4dancers.com
ArtJob Online	www.artjob.org
Backstage.com	www.backstage.com
Casting-America	www.casting-america.com
Casting Daily	www.castingnet.com
Designer Max	www.designermax.com
Electronic Media	www.emonline.com
Entertainment Careers	www.entertainmentcareers.net
EntertainmentJobs.com	www.eej.com
Employment Network	www.employnow.com
Filmbiz.com	www.filmbiz.com
Hollywood Web	www.hollywoodweb.com
Media Communications Association International Job Hotline	www.itva.org/resources/job_hotline.htm
National Association of Broadcasters	www.nab.org
New England Film	www.newenglandfilm.com/jobs.htm
Open Casting.com	www.opencasting.com
Opportunities Online [United Kingdom]	www.opps.co.uk
PlanetSharkProductions.com	www.planetsharkproductions.com
Playbill On-Line	www.playbill.com
Radio Online	www.radio-online.com
Showbizjobs.com	www.showbizjobs.com
Show Biz Data	www.showbizdata.com
Society of Broadcast Engineers	www.sbe.org
Tech TV	www.techtv.com
Theatre Jobs	www.theatrejobs.com
TVjobs.com	www.tvjobs.com
Voice of Dance	www.voiceofdance.com

Help Someone in Transition. ← **WEDDLE's 2004 Job Seeker's Guide.**

Notes
Favorite sites, useful resources

Environmental

Air & Waste Management Association	www.awma.org
American College of Occupational and Environmental Medicine	www.acoem.org
American Water Works Association Career Center (Water Jobs)	www.awwa.org
APSnet-Plant Pathology Online	www.apsnet.org
Earthworks	www.earthworks-jobs.com
EE-Link: The Environmental Education Web Server	www.nceet.snre.umich.edu/jobs.html
EnviroNetwork	www.environetwork.com
EnvironmentalCAREER.com	www.environmentalcareer.com
Environmental Career Opportunities	www.ecojobs.com
Environmental Careers Bulletin Online	www.ecbonline.com
Environmental Careers Organization	www.eco.org
Environmental Careers World	www.environmental-jobs.com
Environmental Construction Engineering Architectural Jobs Online	www.eceajobs.com
Environmental Data Interactive Exchange Job Centre [United Kingdom]	www.edie.net
Environmental Employment Pages	www.datacor.com/jobfair/EnvironmentHome.htm.
Environmental Engineer	www.environmentalengineer.com
Environmental Jobs & Careers	www.ejobs.org
Environmental Nes	www.enn.com
EnviroWorld	www.enviroworld.com
GeoWeb	www.ggrweb.com
GeoWeb Jobs	www.geowebjobs.com
GIS Jobs Clearinghouse	www.gis.umn.edu
GreenBiz.com Joblink	www.greenbiz.com/jobs
Green Dream Jobs	www.sustainablebusiness.com
Job.com	www.job.com/main.html
National Environmental Health Association	www.neha.org
Nevada Mining	www.nevadamining.org
Pollution Online	www.pollutiononline.com
Power Brokers	www.powerbrokersllc.com
Power Online	www.poweronline.com
Public Works	www.publicworks.com
Pulp & Paper Online	www.pulpandpaperonline.com
Solid Waste	www.solidwaste.com
Student Conservation Association	www.thesca.org
TechSavvy.com	www.techsavvy.com
Universities Water Information Network	www.uwin.siu.edu/announce/jobs
Water Online	www.wateronline.com

Find Great Talent. ☛ **WEDDLE's 2004 Recruiter's Guide**

Notes
Favorite sites, useful resources

Equipment Leasing

Equipment Leasing Association	www.elaonline.com
Leasing News	http://64.125.68.90/LeasingNews/JobPosting.htm

Executive/Management

American Bankers Association	www.aba-execjobs.com/index.htm
American College of Healthcare Executives	http://ache.org
American Economic Development Council	www.aedc.org
American Management Association International	www.amanet.org/
American Society of Association Executives Career Headquarters	www.asaenet.org/careerheadquarters
Blue Steps	www.bluesteps.com
Boardseat	www.boardseat.com
CardBrowser.com	www.cardbrowser.com
CareerFile	www.careerfile.com
✵ CareerJournal.com	www.careerjournal.com
CFO.com	www.cfo.com
CFO Publishing	http://cfonet.com
CFO Jobsite	www.cfojobsite.com
Chief Monster	www.chief.monster.com
CIO	www2.cio.com/forums/career/index.cfm
CIO Wanted	http://jobs.cio.com
CM Today	www.cmtoday.com/cmjobs/index.html
Compliance Jobs	www.compliancejobs.com
Corporate Alumni	www.corporatealumni.com
Eclectic [Netherlands]	www.eclectic.nl
Ex Big Five	www.exbigfive.com
Execs on the Net [United Kingdom]	www.eotn.co.uk
✵ ExecuNet	www.execunet.com
Execsearches.com	www.execsearches.com
Executive Openings	www.executiveopenings.com
Executive Registry	www.executiveregistry.com
Executive Taskforce [New Zealand]	http://exectask.co.nz
ExecutiveOpenings.com [United Kingdom]	www.executiveopenings.com
Executive Placement Services	www.execplacement.com
ExecutivesontheWeb.com [United Kingdom]	www.executivesontheweb.com
Financial Executives Institute Career Center	www.fei.org/careers
Ft.com-Financial Times [United Kingdom]	www.ft.com

Notes
Favorite sites, useful resources

Executive/Management (continued)

Futurestep	www.futurestep.com
Global Health Network	www.pit.edu/~super1/index.htm
Humanys.com	www.humanys.com
IMCOR	www.imcor.com
Institute of Management & Administration's Supersite	www.ioma.com
Jobs.ac.uk [United Kingdom]	www.jobs.ac.uk
Monster Execuive	www.executive.monster.com
Net Expat	www.netexpat.com
NetShare	www.netshare.com
RiteSite.com	www.ritesite.com
Score	www.scn.org/civic/score-online
Search Base	www.searchbase.com
Seek Executive [Australia]	http://executive.seek.com.au/index.asp
6FigureJobs.com	www.6figurejobs.com
Stern Alumni Outreach Career	www.stern.nyu.edu
Zhaopin.com [China]	www.zhaopin.com

-F-

Fashion

Atlantic Apparel Contractors Association, Inc.	http://atlanticapparel.com/
Be The 1	www.bethe1.com
Fashion Career Center	www.fashioncareercenter.com
Fashion Group International	www.fgi.org
Fashion Net	www.fashion.net/jobs/positionso.php
Top Fashion Jobs [United Kingdom]	www.topfashionjobs.com/jobs.php

Feminism

Feminist Majority Foundation Online	www.feminist.org
Women's Studies Database	www.inform.umd.edu/EdRes/Topic/WomensStudies

Fiber Optics

The Fiber Optic Association	www.thefoa.org/foajobs.htm
Fiber Optic Marketplace	www.fiberoptic.com/empoppframe.html

Notes
Favorite sites, useful resources

Finance & Accounting (see also Banking, Insurance)

AccountantJobs.com	www.accountantjobs.com
Accountant Jobs Chicago	www.accountantjobschicago.com
AccountManager.com	www.accountmanager.com
Accounting.com	www.accounting.com
Accounting & Finance Jobs	www.accountingjobs.com
Accounting Classifieds	www.accountingclassifieds.com
Accounting Jobs Online	www.accountingjobsonline.com
AccountingNet	www.accountingnet.com
Accounting Professional	www.accountingprofessional.com
Actuary.com	www.actuary.com
AdvancingWomen.net	www.advancingwomen.net
Ambition [Australia]	www.ambition.com.au
American Accounting Association Web Placement Service	http://aaahq.org/placements/default.cfm
American Association for Budget and Program Analysis	www.aabpa.org/employ.html
American Association of Finance & Accounting	www.aafa.com/career.htm
American Association of Hispanic Certified Public Accountants	www.aahcpa.org
American Bankers Association	www.aba.com
American Institute of Certified Public Accountants Career Center	www.cpa2biz.com/Career/default.htm
American Society of Women Accountants Employment Opportunities	www.aswa.org/wanted.html
Annuitiesnot com	www.annuitiesnet.com
Antaeans.com	www.antaeans.com
Argus Clearinghouse	www.clearinghouse.net/index.html
Association of Finance Professionals Career Services	www.afponline.org/careerservices
Association of Latino Professionals in Finance & Accounting Job Postings	www.alpfa.org/profossi/careoppo.asp
Association for Investment Management and Research	www.aimr.com
Audit Jobs Chicago	www.auditjobschicago.com
Audit Net	www.auditnet.org
AuditorJobs.com	www.auditorjobs.com
Awesome Accountants	www.awesomeaccountants.com
BankingBoard.com	www.bankingboard.com
BankJobs	www.bankjobs.com
Bean Brains	www.beanbrains.com
Bloomberg.com	www.bloomberg.com/fun/jobs.html
Big Five Talent	www.bigfivetalent.com

WEDDLE's Helping to Maximize Your ROI ... Your Return on the Internet

Notes
Favorite sites, useful resources

Finance & Accounting (continued)

Bilingual-Jobs	www.bilingual-jobs.com
Bond Buyer	www.bondbuyer.com
Business Finance Magazine	www.businessfinancemag.com
Business-Money Magazine	www.business-money.com
CA Magazine	www.camagazine.com
Canadian Association of Financial Planners	www.cafp.org
Capital Markets Credit Analysts Society Resume Service	www.cmcas.org/resumeservice.asp
CareerBank.com	www.careerbank.com
⛴ CareerJournal.com	www.careerjournal.com
CareerJournal.com Europe	www.careerjournaleurope.com
Careers in Finance	www.careers-in-finance.com
Cash Management Career Center	www.amgi.com
Certified Management Accountants of Canada	www.cma-canada.org
CFO.com	www.cfo.com
CFOEurope.com	www.cfoeurope.com
CFO and CPA Jobs	www.cfoandcpajobs.com
CFO Publishing	http://cfonet.com
Controller Jobs	www.controllerjobs.com
CPA Career Center	www.aicpa.com
CPA Career Solutions [Australia]	www.careers.cpaonline.com.au
CPA Jobs	www.cpajobs.com
CPA Online	www.cpaonline.com/
CPANet	www.cpanet.com
CreditJobs.com	www.creditjobs.com
Degree Hunter	www.degreehunter.com
Doublecuff.com	www.doublecuff.com
Dow Jones Careers	www.dj.com/careers/international/index.html
eFinancial Careers [United Kingdom]	www.efinancialcareers.com
eFinancialCareers.fr [France]	www.efinancialcareer.fr
eFinancial Jobs	www.efinancialjobs.com
Escrowboard.com	www.escrowboard.com
Experience on Demand	www.experienceondemand.com
The Finance Beat	www.search-beat.com/finance.htm
Finance and Commerce	www.finance-commerce.com
Finance Job Network	www.financialjobnet.com
Finance Job Store	www.financejobstore.com
FinanceJobs.com	www.financejobs.com
Finance Wise	www.financewise.com
Financial Executives Institute Career Center	www.fei.org/careers
Financial Executive Networking Group	www.thefeng.org
Financial Job Network	www.fjn.com
FinancialJobs.com	www.financialjobs.com

Notes
Favorite sites, useful resources

Finance & Accounting (continued)

Financial Management Association International Placement Services	www.fma.org/2003placement
Financial Managers Society Career Center	www.fmsinc.org/cms/?pid=1025
Financial Positions	www.financialpositions.com
Financial Women International Careers	www.fwi.org/careers/career.htm
Fortune	www.fortune.com
Ft.com -Financial Times [United Kingdom]	www.ft.com
Fund Raising Jobs	www.fundraisingjobs.com
GAAP Web [United Kingdom]	www.gaapweb.com
Global Association of Risk Professionals Career Center	www.garp.com/ careercenter/index.asp
Global Careers	www.globalcareers.com
iHireAccounting	www.ihireaccounting.com
Illinois CPA Society Career Center	www.icpas.org/icpas/ career-services/carsrce.asp
Institute of Management Accountants Career Center	www.imanet.org/ima/ sec.asp? TRACKID=&CID=12&DID=12
Inside Careers Guide to Chartered Accountancy	www.insidecareers.co.uk
Institute of Chartered Accountants of Alberta	http://206.75.36.123
Institute of Internal Auditors Online Audit Career Center	www.theiia.org/careercenter/ index.cfm
International Association for Registered Financial Planners	www.iarfc.org/ jservices.shtml
Investment Management and Trust Exchange	www.antaeans.com
Jamie's Jobs Finance Professionals Web in California	www.jamiesjobs.com/ s?k=finance&t=1042147302061
JobServe for Accountancy [United Kingdom]	www.accountancy.jobserve.com
✵ jobsinthemoney.com	www.jobsinthemoney.com
Maryland Association of CPAs Job Connect	www.macpa.org/services/ jobconnt/index.htm
MBA Careers	www.mbacareers.com
MBA Free Agents	www.mbafreeagents.com
MBAGlobalNet	www.mbaglobalnet.com
MBAJobs.net	www.mbajobs.net/
MBAmatch.com [England]	www.mbamatch.com
MBA Style Magazine	http://members.aol.com/ mbastyle/web/index.html
Money Careers	www.moneycareers.com/ employers.htm
MortgageBoard.com	www.mortgageboard.com
Mortgage Job Store	www.mortgagejobstore.com
National Association of Black Accountants, Inc. Career Center	www.nabainc. jobcontrolcenter.com

Notes
Favorite sites, useful resources

Finance & Accounting (continued)

National Banking Network	www.banking-financejobs.com
National Black MBA Association, Inc.	www.nbmbaa.org
National Business Employment Weekley	www.employment911.com
National Society of Accountants	www.nsacct.org
National Society of Hispanic MBAs Career Center	www.nshmba.org
NationalJob Network: Financial Jobs Page	www.nationjob.com/financial
National Venture Capital Association	www.nvca.org
New Jersey Society of CPAs	www.njscpa.org
New York Society of Security Analysts Career Resources	www.nyssa.org/jobs
New York State Society of CPAs	www.nysscpa.org/classified/main.cfm
Real Estate Finance Jobs	www.realestatefinancejobs.com
Risk & Insurance Management Society Careers	www.rims.org/Template.cfm?Section=JobBank1&Template=/Jobbank/SearchJobForm.cfm
Global Association of Risk Professionals Career Center	www.garp.com/careercenter/index.asp
Search Beat	www.search-beat.com/finance.htm
Securities Industry Association Career Resource Center	www.sia.com/career
Smart Money	www.smartmoney.com
Society of Actuaries	www.soa.org
Society of Risk Analysis Opportunities	www.sra.org/opptys.php
Street Jobs	www.streetjobs.com
Tax Jobs	www.taxjobs.com
Tax Jobs Chicago	www.taxjobschicago.com
Tax-Talent.com	www.tax-talent.com
Tennessee Society of CPA's Job Listings	www.tscpa.com/public/classifieds.htm
Titleboard.com	www.titleboard.com
Toronto Society of Financial Analysts [Canada]	www.tsfa.ca
UnderwritingJobs.com	www.uwjobs.com

Funeral Industry

FuneralNet	www.funeralnet.com
National Funeral Directors Association	www.nfda.org

Looking for a new or better job?   Looking for top talent?
Use WEDDLE's publications. See the Catalog in this book.

Notes
Favorite sites, useful resources

WEDDLE's Helping to Maximize Your ROI ... Your Return on the Internet

-G-

Gaming

Casino Careers Online   www.casinocareers.com
Game Jobs   www.gamejobs.com

General

555-1212	www.555-1212.com
About Jobs	www.aboutjobs.com
Abracat	www.abracat.com
ActiJob	www.actijob.com
Action Jobs	www.actionjobs.com
Adguide's Employment Web Site	www.adguide.com
Adquest 3D	www.adquest3d.com/main.cfm
Adsearch	www.adsearch.com
Best Local Jobs	www.bestlocaljobs.com
Advancing Women	www.advancingwomen.com
AECPII	www.aecpii.com
Alianza (Latino)	www.alianza.org
Alta Vista Job Center	http://204.123.9.98
America's Employers	www.americasemployers.com
⚐ America's Job Bank	www.ajb.dni.us
American City Business Journals	www.bizjournalshire.com
AmericanJobs.com	www.americanjobs.com
American Preferred Jobs	www.preferredjobs.com
AmpleJobs	www.amplejobs.com
Ants.com	www.ants.com
Any Who	www.anywho.com
Area Jobs	www.areajobs.com
Asia-Net	www.asia-net.com
Association Job Source	www.jobsourcenetwork.com/assoc.html
Available Jobs	www.avallablejobs.com
Beaucoup!	www.beaucoup.com/1geneng.html
Best.com	www.best.com/index1.shtml
⚐ Best Jobs USA	www.bestjobsusa.com
BigJobs.net	www.bigjobs.net
Black Career Women Online	www.bcw.org
THE BLACK COLLEGIAN Online	www.blackcollegian.com
Blue Collar Jobs	www.bluecollarjobs.com
Boldface Jobs	www.boldfacejobs.com
Boston Globe	www.globe.com
Branch Staff Online	www.branchstaffonline.com

Notes
Favorite sites, useful resources

General (continued)

Business Week Online	www.businessweek.com/careers
Call Center Ops	www.callcenterops.com
Career.com	www.career.com
◼ CareerBuilder	www.careerbuilder.com
CareerBuzz.com	www.careerbuzz.com
CareerCast	www.careercast.com
Career Center	www.careercenter.com
CareerChase	www.careerchase.net
The Career Connection	www.connectme.com
Career Engine	www.careerengine
Career Exchange	www.careerexchange.com
CareerExposure	www.careerexposure.com
Careerfile.com	www.careerfile.com
Career Flex	www.careerflex.com
Career Giant	www.careergiant.com
◼ CareerJournal.com	www.careerjournal.com
Career Magazine	www.careermag.com
CareerMart	www.careermart.com
Career Pal	www.careerpal.com
Career Resource Center	www.careers.org
CareerShop	www.careershop.com
Career Site	www.careersite.com
Career Span	http://careerspan.com
Careers.org	www.careers.org
Career Surf	http://careersurf.com
Career Talk	www.careertalk.com
CareersMVP.com	www.careersmvp.com
Chain Store Guide	www.csgis.com
Chattanooga Publishing	www.chatpub.com
Chowk	www.chowk.com
City Search.com	www.citysearch.com
Classifieds 2000	www.classifieds2000.com
Community Associations Institute	www.caionline.org
Contract Employment Connection	www.ntes.com
Contract-Jobs.com	www.contract-jobs.com
◼ CraigsList	www.craigslist.org
Creative Hotlist	www.creativehotlist.com
Customer Service Management	www.csm-us.com
Customer Service University	www.customerserviceuniversity.com
Daily Digest	www.le-digest.com
Database America	www.databaseamerica.com
Delphi Forums	www.delphi.com/windowforjobs
DirectEmployers	www.directemployers.com
Direct Job	www.directjob.com

Notes
Favorite sites, useful resources

General (continued)

Direct-jobs.com	www.direct-jobs.com
Direct Mail	www.the-dma.org/cgi/jbsearch
Diversity Careers	www.diversitycareers
Diversity Employment	www.diversityemployment.com
DiversityLink	www.diversitylink.com
Diversity Search	www.diversitysearch.com
e-learning Jobs	www.e-learningjobs.com
ePage Internet Classifieds	http://ep.com
eCom Recruitment	www.ecomrecruitment.com
eJobResource.com	www.ejobresource.com
Employers Online	www.employersonline.com
Employmax	www.employmax.com
Employment	www.employment.com
Employment 911	www.employment911.com
★ EmploymentGuide.com	www.employmentguide.com
Employment Spot	www.employmentspot.com
Employment Weekly	www.employment-weekly.com
Employment Wizard	www.employmentwizard.com
eNeighborhoods	www.enighborhoods.com/productsservices.htm
The EPages Classifieds	www.ep.com
Experience on Demand	www.experienceondemand.com
Finder2000	www.finder2000.com
First Market Research	http://firstmarket.com
★ FlipDog.com	www.flipdog.com
4 Work	www.4work.com
Fresh Jobs	www.freshjobs.com
Fun Jobs	www.funjobs.com
Future Access Employment Guide	www.futureaccess.com
Garage.com	www.garage.com
Get A Job	www.getajob.com
Get Jobs	www.getjobs.com
Go Ferret Go	www.goferretgo.com
Go Jobs	www.gojobs.com
Google.com	www.google.com
Got A Job	www.gotajob.com
Grass is Greener	www.grassisgreener.com
Group Web	http://groupweb.com/opening/jobs.htm
The Help Wanted Page	www.helpwantedpage.com
Help-Wanted.net	www.help-wanted.net
Hire.com	www.hire.com
Hire Web	www.hireweb.com
Hiring Network	www.hiringnetwork.com
Hiring Online	www.hiringonline.com

Notes
Favorite sites, useful resources

General (continued)

Homefair	www2.homefair.com
How2FindAJob.com	www.how2findajob.com
☒ HotJobs	www.hotjobs.com
Hot Resumes	www.hotresumes.com
Hennepin County Job Openings	www.co.hennepin.mn.us/jobs/jobs.htm
123hire.com	www.123hire.com
Hiregate.com	www.hiregate.com
HispanicBusiness.com	www.hispanicbusiness.com
100 Hot	www.100hot.com/jobs
Hottest 100 Job Sites	www.worldhot.com
HRpal.com	www.hrpal.com
Human-Intelligence.com	www.human-intelligence.com
iHireJobNetwork	www.iHireJobNetwork.com
I Want a New Job	www.currents.net/resources/iwantanewjob/index.html
Ideal Jobs.com	www.idealjobs.com
InfoSpace.com	www.infospace.com
Insta Match	www.instamatch.com
International Career Employment Center	www.internationaljobs.org
International Customer Service Association Job Board	http://secure2.neology.com/ICSA/jobs/employer/welcome.cfm
Internet Career Connection	www.iccweb.com
The Internet Job Locator	www.joblocator.com/jobs
Internet Traffic Report	www.internettrafficreport.com
Iowa Smart Idea	www.smartcareermove.com
I-resign.com	www.i-resign.com
Its Your Job Now	www.itsyourjobnow.com
Job AA	www.jobaa.com
Job Ads1	www.jobads1.com
Job Animal	www.jobanimal.com
JobBank USA	www.jobbankusa.com
Job Catalog	www.jobcatalog.com
JobCenterUSA.com	www.jobcenterusa.com
Job Choices	www.jobweb.org/jconline
Job City USA.com	www.jobcityusa.com
Job.com	www.job.com
Job Exchange	www.jobexchange.com
JobFind.Com	www.jobfind.com
Job Fly	www.jobfly.com
Job Front	www.jobfront.com
Job-Hunt	www.job-hunt.org
Job Hunt	www.jobhunt.com
Jobing.com	www.jobing.com
Job Land Virtual Classifieds	http://jobland.com/classifieds

Notes
Favorite sites, useful resources

General (continued)

Job Launch	www.joblaunch.com
Job Lynx	http://joblynx.com
The Job Market	www.thejobmarket.com
Job Master	www.rvp.com/jh
Job Match	www.jobmatch.com
Job Options	www.joboptions.com
Jobs+	www.jobsplus.org
Jobs America	www.us.plusjobs.com
Jobs Online	www.jobsonline.com
Jobs-Online	www.jobs-online.net
Job Point Connection	www.jobpoint.com
Job Safari	www.jobsafari.com
Job SAT	www.jobsat.com
Job-Search-Engine	www.job-search-engine.com
Job Sleuth	www.jobsleuth.com
Job Sniper	www.jobsniper.com
Job Star	www.jobstar.org
Job Trak	www.jobtrak.com
Jobvertise	www.jobvertise.com
Job Warehouse	www.jobw.com
1 to 1 jobs.com	www.1to1jobs.com
Jobs Inc.	www.jobsinc.com
JobPilot.com	www.ja-usa.com
Jobs at Corporations	www.searchbeat.com/jobs2.htm
Jobs-Careers	www.jobs-careers.com
Jobs Made Easy	www.jobsmadeeasy.com
Jobs on the Web	www.jobsontheweb.com
Jobs Posted Free	www.jobspostedfree.com
Jumbo Classifieds	www.jumboclassifieds.com
LatinoWeb	www.latinoweb.com
LatPro	www.latpro.com
Liszt	www.liszt.com
LocalOpenings.com	www.localopenings.com
Local Staff	www.localstaff.com
Lycos City Guide	http://cityguide.lycos.com/usa
Mail.com	http://corp.mail.com
MegaJobSites	www.megajobsites.com
Meta Crawler	www.go2net.com/search.html
Minorities Job Bank	www.iminorities.com
Minority Career Network	www.minoritycareernet.com
Monitor	www.monitordaily.com
⊠ Monster.com	www.monster.com
My Job Search	www.myjobsearch.com
The Nando Times	www.nandotimes.com
National Diversity Newspaper Job Bank	www.newsjobs.com

Notes
Favorite sites, useful resources

General (continued)

⚐ NationJob Network	www.nationjob.com
Nationwide Consultants	www.nationwideconsultants.com
Neighbor Works Net	www.nw.org
NetNoir	www.netnoir.com
⚐ Net-Temps	www.net-temps.com
NowHiring.com	www.nowhiring.com
Online-Jobs	www.online-jobs.com
Only-Jobs	www.only-jobs.com
People Bank	www.peoplebank.com/pbank/owa/pbk06w00.main
People Bonus	www.peoplebonus.com
Personnel Department	www.careermachine.com
Personnel Desk	www.personneldesk.com
PickaJob.com	www.pickajob.com
Planet Recruit	www.planetrecruit.com
Position Filler	www.positionfiller.com
Position Watch	www.positionwatch.com
Pro Hire.com	www.prohire.com
Quintessential Careers	www.quintcareers.com
RecruiterConnection	www.recruiterconnection.com
Recruiting Shark	www.recruitingshark.com
⚐ RegionalHelpWanted.com	www.regionalhelpwanted.com
Rep Resources	www.represources.com
ResourceOcean.com	www.resourceocean.com
Resume Blaster	www.resumeblaster.com
ResumeXPRESS	www.resumexpress.com
Resume Innovations	www.resume-innovations.com
Resume' Net	www.resumenet.com
ResumeRabbit.com	www.resumerabbit.com
Resumes at iquest	http://web.iquest.net/reg-recar/resumes.htm
Resumes on the Web	www.resweb.com
Resunet	www.resunet.com
RetiredBrains	www.retiredbrains.com
Salary.com	www.salary.com
Saludos Web Site	www.saludos.com
Search Ease	www.searchease.com
See Me Resumes	www.seemeresumes.com
Select Minds	www.selectminds.com
The Sense Media Surfer	http://sensemedia.net/employment.edge
Skill Hunter	www.skillhunter.com
Start Up Jobs	www.startupjobs.com
Start Up Zone	www.startupzone.com
Starting Point	www.stpt.com/default.asp

WEDDLE's Helping to Maximize Your ROI ... Your Return on the Internet

Notes
Favorite sites, useful resources

General (continued)

State Jobs	http://statejobs.com
The Sunday Paper	www.sundaypaper.com
SwapJobs.com	www.swapjobs.com
Switchboard	www.switchboard.com
TargetedJobSites.com	www.targetedjobsites.com
Team Rewards	www.careerrewards.com
TelecommutingJobs	www.tjobs.com
Teleplaza	www.teleplaza.com
Thingama Job	www.thingamajob.com
TopJobs USA	www.topjobsusa.com
Totaljobs.com	www.totaljobs.com
Tripod	http://members.tripod.com
⚠ TrueCareers	www.truecareers.com
Union Jobs Clearinghouse	www.unionjobs.com
United States Department of Labor	www.dol.gov
UpSeek	www.upseek.com
US Jobs	www.usjobs.com
USA Hot Jobs	www.usahotjobs.com
USJobNet.com	www.usjobnet.com
⚠ Vault.com	www.vault.com
Vertical Net	www.verticalnet.com
Virtual Job Fair	www.jobcenter.com
Virtual Recruiting Network	www.dmpmail.com
Virtual Resume	www.virtualresume.com/vitae
Web Crawler	www.webcrawler.com
Web Reference	www.webreference.com/
Wetfeet	www.wetfeet.com
Womenswire	www.womenswire.com
Work at Home Digest	www.intlhomeworkers.com
WorkLife.com	www.worklife.com
Work-Web	www.work-web.com
The World Wide Web Employment Office	www.employmentoffice.net
WorldWorkz.com	www.worldworkz.com
Yahoo Careers	http://careers.yahoo.com
Yahoo's Classifieds	http://classifieds.yahoo.com
Yep.com	www.yep.com

Graphic Arts/Electronic & Traditional (See also Journalism & Media)

3D Café	www.3dcafe.com
3Dmax	www.3dmax.com
3DSite	www.3dsite.com
Adrecruiter	www.adrecruiter.com
Advertising-PR.com	www.advertising-pr.com
American Institute of Graphic Arts	www.aiga.org

Notes
Favorite sites, useful resources

Graphic Arts/Electronic & Traditional (continued)

Communication Arts Magazine	www.commarts.com
Communications Round Table	www.roundtable.org
Coroflot	www.coroflot.com
Creative Focus	www.focusstaff.com
Design Management Institute Job Bank	www.designmgt.org/dmi/html/jobbank/jobbank_d.jsp
Design Sphere Online Job Hunt	www.dsphere.net
Desktop Publishing	http://desktoppublishing.com
FindCreative.com	www.findcreative.com
Freelance BBS	www.freelancebs.com
Graphic Artists Guild JobLine	www.gag.org/jobline/index.html
Graphic Artists Information Network	www.gain.org
Graphic Artists Monthly	www.gammag.com
Interior Design Jobs	www.interiordesignjobs.com
Media Lab	www.media.mit.edu
Media Street.com	www.mediastreet.com
Mip Map	www.mipmap.com
National Assocation of Printing Ink Manufacturers	www.napim.org
New York New Media Association	www.nynma.com/jobs
Portfolios.com	www.portfolios.com
Print Jobs	www.printjobs.com
Printing Careers	www.printingcareers.com
Screenprinting & Graphic Imaging Association International	www.sgia.org/employ/employ.html
Silicon Alley	www.siliconalley.com/sa/index.cfm

-H-

Healthcare/Medical

Administration/Management

American College of Healthcare Executives	http://aohc.org
College of Healthcare Information Management Executives	www.chime-net.org/crc/job/job.htm
Healthline Management	www.hmistl.com
Medbizpeople.com	www.medbizpeople.com
Medical Case Management Jobs	www.cascmanagementjobs.com

Looking for a new or better job?   Looking for top talent?
Use WEDDLE's publications. See the Catalog in this book.

Notes
Favorite sites, useful resources

Healthcare/Medical (continued)

Acute Care/Critical Care/Intensive Care
American Association of Critical Care Nurses	www.aacn.org
JobAcuteCare.com	www.jobacutecare.com
JobCriticalCare.com	www.jobcriticalcare.com
JobICU.com	www.jobicu.com
JobIntensiveCare.com	www.jobintensivecare.com

Addiction/Substance Abuse
Addiction Medicine Jobs	www.addictionmedicinejobs.com
Substance Abuse Jobs	www.substanceabusejobs.com

Anethesiology
Gas Jobs	www.gasjobs.com
GasWorks.com	www.gasworks.com

Cardiology
Cardiologist Jobs	www.cardiologistjobs.com
JobCardiology.com	www.jobcardiology.com

Equipment-Health
Jobaids.com	www.jobaids.com
MDL Career Center	http://careercenter.devicelink.com

Healthcare-General
Absolutely Healthcare	www.healthjobsusa.com
Allied Health Jobs	www.alliedhealthjobs.com
Allied Health Opportunities Directory	www.gvpub.com
America's Health Care Source	www.healthcaresource.com
Centers for Disease Control	www.cdc.gov
Discover Jobs	www.discoverjobs.com
Employ Med	www.embbs.com/jobs/jobs.html
Find Medical	www.findmedical.com
Future Mcd	http://ourworld.compuserve.com/homepages/futuremed/main.htm
GovMedCareers.com	www.govmedcareers.com
Healthcare Hub	www.healthcarehub.com
Health Care Jobs Online	www.hcjobsonline.com
Health Care Mart	www.healthcaremart.com
Health Care Match	www.healthcarematch.com
Health Care Hiring	www.healthcarehiring.com
Healthcare/Monster	www.healthcare.monster.com
HealthCareRecruitment.com	www.healthcarerecruitment.com
Health Care Seeker	www.healthcareseeker.com
Health Careers	www.healthcareers-online.com

Notes
Favorite sites, useful resources

Healthcare/Medical (continued)
Healthcare-General (continued)

Health Direction	www.healthdirection.com
HealthJobsite.com	www.healthjobsite.com
HealthJobsUSA.com	www.healthjobsusa.com
Health Network USA	www.hnusa.com
Health Seek.com	www.healthseek.com
HealthCare Job Store	www.healthcarejobstore.com
Healthcare Professional Jobs	www.HealthcareProfessional.com
Healthcare Source	www.healthcareresource.com
HealthCareerWeb.com	www.healthcareerweb.com
Healthecareers	www.artofsearch.com
HealthOpps	www.healthopps.com
HireBio.com	www.hirebio.com
HireRX.com	www.hirerx.com
HireMedical.com	www.hiremedical.com
HireNursing.com	www.hirenursing.com
HireCentral.com	www.hirecentral.com
JobAlliedHealth.com	www.joballiedhealth.com
JobHealthCareers.com	www.jobhealthcareers.com
JobMedical.com	www.jobmedical.com
Jobscience Network	www.jobscience.com
Job Span	www.jobspan.com
JobsinHealth [Ireland]	www.jobsinhealth.ie
Jobs in Healthcare	www.jobsinhealthcare.com
Med Bulletin	www.m3jobs.com/jobsearch2.php
Med Careers	www.medcareers.com
Med Connect	www.medconnect.com
Medhunters	www.medhunters.com
MedicSolve.com [United Kingdom]	www.medicsolve.com
MedLaunch	www.medlaunch.com
MedMarket	www.medical-admart.com
Medical AdMart	www.medical-admart.com
Medical Design Online	www.medicaldesignonline.com
Medical Matrix	www.medmatrix.org/index.asp
Medical Words	www.md123.com
Medicenter.com	www.medicenter.com
Medi Match	www.medimatch.com
Medi-Smart	www.medi-smart.com/renal4.htm
Medimorphus.com	www.medimorphus.com
MEDSTER.com	www.medster.com
✦ Medzilla	www.medzilla.com
Modern Healthcare	www.modernhealthcare.com
National Association for Health Care Recruitment	www.nahcr.com
The National Assembly	www.nassembly.org
New England Journal of Medicine	www.nejm.org

Notes
Favorite sites, useful resources

WEDDLE's Helping to Maximize Your ROI … Your Return on the Internet

Healthcare/Medical (continued)
Hospital-General
Arizona Hospital and Healthcare Association AZHealthJobs	www.azhha.org
Colorado Health and Hospital Association	www.cha.com
HMonster.com	www.hmonster.com
Hospital Hub	www.hospitaljobweb.com
Hospital Jobs Online	www.hospitaljobsonline.com
HospitalSoup.com	www.hospitalsoup.com
Hospital Web	http://neuro-www.mgh harvard.edu/hospitalweb.shtml
JobHospital.com	www.jobhospital.com
MedBizPeople.com	www.medbizpeople.com

International
CanMed [Canada]	www.canmed.com
DERWeb [United Kingdom]	www.derweb.co.uk
EMBL Job Vacancies [Germany]	www.embl-heidelberg.de/ExternalInfo/Jobs
Global Health Network	http://info.pitt.edu/HOME/GHNet/GHNet.html
HUM-MOLGEN [Germany]	www.informatik.uni-rostock.ed/HUM-MOLGEN/anno/position.html
Medjobsuk.com [United Kingdom]	www.medjobsuk.com
Opportunities Online [United Kingdom]	www.opps.co.uk

Midwife
JobMidwife.com	www.jobmidwife.com
MidwifeJobs	www.midwifejobs.com
NMC4Jobs.com [United Kingdom]	www.nmc4jobs.com
Professional Information from the American College of Nurse-Midwives	www.midwife.org

Nurses/Nursing
AllNurses.com	www/allnurses.com
American Association of Critical Care Nurses	www.aacn.org
American Nurses Association	www.nursingworld.org
ANNAlink	http://anna.inurse.com
Association of Perioperative Registered Nurses Online Career Center	www.aorn.org/Careers/default.htm
GraduateNurse.com	www.graduatenurse.com
Guaranteed Employment Advertising & Resume Service	www.nurse-recruiter.com
HealthJobsUSA.com	www.healthjobsusa.com

Notes
Favorite sites, useful resources

WEDDLE's Helping to Maximize Your ROI ... Your Return on the Internet

Healthcare/Medical (continued)
Nurses/Nursing (continued)
HireNursing.com	www.hirenursing.com
Hot Nurse Jobs	www.hotnursejobs.com
iHireNursing.com	www.ihirenursing.com
JobCNA.com	www.jobcna.com
JobLPN.com	www.joblpn.com
JobLVN.com	www.joblvn.com
JobNurse.com	www.jobnurse.com
JobNursePractitioner.com	www.jobnursepractitioner.com
JobNursingAid.com	www.jobnursingaid.com
JobPracticalNurse.com	www.jobpracticalnurse.com
JobPracticioner.com	www.jobpracticioner.com
JobRN.com	www.jobrn.com
JobStaffNurse.com	www.jobstaffnurse.com
Locum Tenens	www.locumtenens.com
National Association of Hispanic Nurses	
Houston Chapter	www.nahnhouston.org
Nurse Career	www.nursecareer.com
Nurse Director Jobs	www.directorofnursingjobs.com
Nurse Manager Jobs	www.nursemanagerjobs.com
Nurse Zone	www.nursezone.com
Nurseserve [United Kingdom]	www.nurseserv.co.uk
Nurses for a Healthier Tomorrow	www.nursesource.org
Nursing Center	www.nursingcenter.com
Nursing Hands	www.nursinghands.com
NursingJobs.com	www.nursingjobs.com
NursingMatters.com	www.nursingmatters.com
Nursing Spectrum Career Fitness Online	www.nursingspectrum.com
PDCforNurses.com	www.pdcfornurses.com
Psychiatric Nurse Jobs	www.psychiatricnursejobs.com
RN.com	www.rn.com
TravelNursing.com	www.travelnursing.com

OBGYN
JobOBGYN.com	www.jobobgyn.com
Obstetric Jobs	www.obstetricjobs.com

Pediatrics
JobPediatrics.com	www.jobpediatrics.com
Pediatric Jobs	www.pediatricjobs.com

Pharmacist/Pharmacy (See also Pharmaceutical)
American Pharaceutical Association	www.aphanet.org
Association for Applied Human Pharmacology	
[Germany]	www.agah-web.de

Notes
Favorite sites, useful resources

Healthcare/Medical (continued)
Pharmacist/Pharmacy (continued)
Cen-ChemJobs.org	www.cen-chemjobs.org
HireRX.com	www.hirerx.com
iHirePharmacy.com	www.ihirepharmacy.com
Pharmaceutical Rep Jobs	www.pharmaceuticalrepjobs.com
RPh on the Go	www.rphonthego.com
RPhRecruiter	www.rphrecruiter.com
RxCareerCenter	www.rxcareercenter.com
Rx Immigration	www.rximmigration.com
RxWebportal	www.rxwebportal.com

Physical Therapy/Occupational Therapy
American College of Occupational and Environmental Medicine	www.acoem.org
American Occupational Therapy Association	www.aota.org
American Physical Therapy Association	www.apta.org
American Society of Clinical Pharmacology and Therapeutics	www.ascpt.org
Physical Therapist Jobs	www.physicaltherapistjobs.com
PT Central	www.ptcentral.com
Rehab Options	www.rehaboptions.com

Physicians
Academic Physician & Scientist	www.acphysci.com
American Medical Association Journal of the AMA (JAMA) Physician Recruitment Ads	www.ama-assn.org/sci-pubs/md_recr/md_recr
Doc Job	www.docjob.com
Doc on the Web	www.webdoc.com
DoctorWork.com	www.doctorwork.com
Ed Physician	www.edphysician.com
iHirePhysicians.com	www.ihirephysicians.com
JobMD.com	www.jobmd.com
JobPhysician.com	www.jobphysician.com
MD Job Site	www.mdjobsite.com
Physician Work	www.physicianwork.com
Physician's Employment	www.physemp.com
Practice Link	www.practicelink.com
Web MD	www.webmd.com

Psychology/Psychiatry/Mental Health
American Psychological Association Monitor Classified Advertising	www.apa.org/ads
American Psychological Society ObserverJob Listings	www.psychologicalscience.org

Notes
Favorite sites, useful resources

Healthcare/Medical (continued)
Psychology/Psychiatry/Mental Health (continued)

American Psychological Society	www.hanover.edu/psych/aps/aps.html
iHireMentalHealth.com	www.ihirementalhealth.com
iHireTherapy.com	www.ihiretherapy.com
JobPsychiatry.com	www.jobpsychiatry.com
JobPsychology.com	www.jobpsychology.com
Mental Health Jobs	www.mentalhealthjobs.com
Mental Health Net	www.cmhc.com/wwwboard/bb2.htm
Mental Health Net	www.mentalhelp.net
National Association Of School Psychologists	www.naspcareercenter.org
Psychiatric Nurse Jobs	www.psychiatricnursejobs.com
Psychiatrist Jobs	www.psychiatristjobs.com
Psychologist Jobs	www.psychologistjobs.com
Social Psychology Network	www.socialpsychology.org

Research

American Society for Clinical Laboratory Science	www.ascls.org
American Society for Clinical Pathology	www.ascp.org
American Society of Clinical Pharmacology and Therapeutics	www.ascpt.org
Association for Applied Human Pharmacology [Germany]	www.agah-web.de
Association of Clinical Research in the Pharmaceutical Industry [United Kingdom]	www.acrpi.com
Association of Clinical Reseach Professionals Career Center	www.acrpnet.org
BC Biotechnology Alliance [Canada]	www.biotech.bc.ca/bcba
BioStaticianjobs.com	www.biostaticianjobs.com
Biotechemployment.com	www.biotechemployment.com
Biotechnology Industry Organization	www.bio.org/welcome.html
Canadian Society of Biochemistry and Mollecular and Cellular Biologists Experimental Medicine Job Listing	www.medcor.mcgill.ca/EXPMED/DOCS/jobs.html
History of Science Society	http.//depts.washington.edu/hssexec
Texas Healthcare & Bioscience Institute	www.thbi.org

Specialties-Other

American Association of Medical Assistants	www.aama-ntl.org
American Association of Respiratory Care	www.aarc.org
American College of Occupational and Environmental Medicine	www.acoem.org
American Industrial Hygiene Association	www.aiha.org

Notes
Favorite sites, useful resources

Healthcare/Medical (continued)
Specialties-Other (continued)

American Society of Ichthyologists and Herpetologists	http://199.245.200.110/
CancerJobs.net [United Kingdom]	www.cancerjobs.net
iHireMedicalSecretaries.com	www.ihiremedicalsecretaries.com
iHireMedTechs.com	www.ihiremedtechs.com
iHireNutrition.com	www.ihirenutrition.com
iHireRadiology.com	www.ihireradiology.com
JobDiagnostics.com	www.jobdiagnostics.com
JobDietician.com	www.jobdietician.com
JobEKG.com	www.jobekg.com
JobEmergency.com	www.jobemergency.com
JobERJobHealthcare.com	www.joberjobhealthcare.com
JobHematology.com	www.jobhematology.com
JobHomeHealth.com	www.jobhomehealth.com
JobHospice.com	www.jobhomehealth.com
JobImaging.com	www.jobimaging.com
JobImmunology.com	www.jobimmunology.com
JobLaboratory.com	www.joblaboratory.com
JobMedTech.com	www.jobmedtech.com
JobsMRI.com	www.jobsmri.com
JobNeonatal.com	www.jobneonatal.com
JobOncology.com	www.joboncology.com
Job Opportunities in Entomology	www.colostate.edu/Depts/
JobParamedic.com	www.jobparamedic.com
JobPathology.com	www.jobpathology.com
JobPrimaryCare.com	www.jobprimarycare.com
JobRadiology.com.com	www.jobradiology.com
JobSurgeon.com	www.jobsurgeon.com
JobTelemetry.com	www.jobtelemetry.com
JobTherapy.com	www.jobtherapy.com/ Entomology/jobs/jobs.html
JobTransplant.com	www.jobtransplant.com
JobX-ray.com	www.jobx-ray.com
MedBizPeople.com	www.medbizpeople.com
Medical Consultants Network	www.mcn.com
Medical Sales Jobs.com	www.medicalsalesjobs.com
Medical Secretary Jobs.com	www.medicalsecretary.com
National Environmental Health Association	www.neha.org
NukeWorker.com	www.nukeworker.com
Radiological Society of North America	www.rsna.org
Renal World	www.renalworld.com

Help Someone in Transition. ☛ **WEDDLE's 2004 Job Seeker's Guide.**

Notes
Favorite sites, useful resources

Healthcare/Medical (continued)
Students/Recent Graduates
Career Espresso — www.sph.emory.edu/studentservice

The College of Education & Human Development at the University of Minnesota — http://education.umn.edu/sps/career
Degree Hunter — www.degreehunter.com

High Tech/Technical/Technology

The Ada Project — www.cs.yale.edu/homes/tap/tap.html
AmericanJobs.com — www.americanjobs.com
Association for Educational Communications and Technology Job Center — www.aect.org
Career Net — www.careernet.com
Contract Employment Weekly — www.ceweekly.com
High Technology Careers — www.hightechcareers.com
Infoworks - The Computer Job Center — www.IT123.com
Job Authority — www.jobauthority.com
Job Searching - Technical — http://jobsearchtech.miningco.com
Metro Atlanta High Tech Personnel Association — http://mahtpa.hom.mindspring.com
New Dimensions in Technology, Inc. — www.ndt.com
New Mexico High Tech Job Forum — www.nmtechjobs.com
Passport Access — www.passportaccess.com
Society for Technical Communications — www.stc.org/post_job.html
TechJobsOnline.com — www.techjobsonline.com
TechJobsScotland — www.techjobsscotland.com
Technical Recruiter — www.technicalrecruiter.com
TechResults — www.techresults.com
US Tech Jobs — www.ustechjobs.net
Virtual Job Fair — www.careerexpo.com

Hospitality (See also Culinary/Food Preparation)

Avero — www.averoinc.com/
Careers in Food — www.careersinfood.com
Casino Careers Online — www.casinocareers.com
Cooljobs — http://cooljobs.com
CoolWorks.com — www.coolworks.com
Executive Placement Services — www.execplacement.com
Food and Drink Jobs — www.foodanddrinkjobs.com
FoodIndustryJobs.com — www.foodindustryjobs.com
Hcareers — www.hcareers.com

Notes
Favorite sites, useful resources

Hospitality (continued)

HospitalityAdventures.com	www.hospitalityadventures.com
Hospitality Net Virtual Job Exchange [Netherlands]	www.hospitalitynet.nl
Hospitality Online	www.hospitalityonline.com
Hotel Jobs	www.hoteljobs.com
Hotel Jobs Network	www.hoteljobsnetwork.com
Hotel-Restaurant Jobs	www.hotel-restaurantjobs.com
iHireHospitality.com	www.ihirehospitality.com
iHireHospitalityServices.com	www.ihirehospitalityservices.com
International Association of Conference Centers Online	www.iacconline.com/home.cfm
Job Monkey	www.jobmonkey.com
Lifeguardingjobs.com	www.lifeguardingjobs.com
MeetingJobs.com	www.meetingjobs.com
Museum Jobs	www.museumjobs.com
Resortjobs.co.uk [United Kingdom]	www.resortjobs.co.uk
Restaurant Careers	www.restaurant-careers.com
Restaurant Job Site	www.restaurantjobsite.com
Restaurant Jobs	www.restaurantjobs.com
Restaurant Mangement Jobs	www.restaurantmgmtjobs.com
Restaurant Manager Job Site	www.restaurantmgrjobsite.com
Showbizjobs.com	www.showbizjobs.com
SkiingtheNet	www.skiingthenet.com
StarChefs	www.starchefs.com

Hourly Workers (see also Classifieds-Newspaper)

⚑ EmploymentGuide.com	www.employmentguide.com
Monster JobMatch	www.jobmatch.com
YouApplyHere.com	www.youapplyhere.com

Human Resources

American Evaluation Association	www.eval.org
American Society for Training & Development Job Bank	http://jobs.astd.org
American Management Association International	www.amanet.org/start.htm
Argus Clearinghouse	www.clearinghouse.net/index.html
Atlanta Human Resources Association	www.ahraonline.com/
BenefitsLink	www.benefitslink.com
Cable and Telecommunications Human Resources Association	www.cthra.com
Career Center for Workforce Diversity	www.eop.com

Notes
Favorite sites, useful resources

Human Resources (continued)

Careers On-Line	http://disserv.stu.umn.edu
Central Iowa Chapter, SHRM	http://cishrm.org/
Chesapeake Human Resources Association	www.chra.com
College and University Personnel Association JobLine	www.cupa.org/jobline/jobline.htm
Dallas Human Resource Management Association	www.dallashr.org
Employease	www.eease.com
Houston Human Resource Management Association	www.hhrma.org/default.shtml
HRCareersUSA.com	www.hrcareersusa.com
hrcomm	www.hrcomm.com
HR Connections	www.hrjobs.com
HR Job Net	www.hrjobnet.com
HR-Jobs	www.hr-jobs.net
HR Net	www.the-hrnet.com
HR Next	www.hrnext.com
HR Pro Online	www.hrproonline.com
HR Professionals	http://hrpro.org/main.html
HR Recruiting	http://hr-recruiting.com
HR Staffers	www.hrstaffers.com
HR World	www.hrworld.com
HRIM Mall	www.hrimmall.com
HRM Jobs	www.hrmjobs.com
HRMA Resource Bank	www.hrma.org/bank
HRS Jobs	www.hrsjobs.com
Human Resource Association of Broward County	www.hrabc.org
Human Resource Association of Central Indiana	www.hraci.org
Human Resource Association of Greater Kansas City	http://hrma-kc.org
Human Resource Association of Greater Oak Brook	http://members.aol.com/hraob/main.htm
Human Resource Association of the National Capital Area Job Bank Listing	http://hra-nca.org/job_list.asp
Human Resource Association of New York	www.nyshrm.org
Human Resource Independent Consultants (HRIC) On-Line Job Leads	www.hric.org/hric/hrcaopp1.html
Human Resource Management Association of Mid Michigan Job Postings	http://hrmamm.com/jobs.asp
Human Resource Professionals	www.hrxperts.org
Human Resources Online [Russia]	www.hro.ru
Human Resources.org	www.humanresources.org

Notes
Favorite sites, useful resources

Human Resources (continued)

iHireHR.com	www.ihirehr.com
International Foundation of Employee Benefit Plans Job Postings	www.ifebp.org/jobs/default.asp
Instructional Systems Technology Jobs	http://education.indiana.edu/ist/students/jobs/joblink.html
International Association for Human Resource Information Management Job Central	http://ihr.hrdpt.com
Independent Human Resource Consultants Association	www.ihrca.com/Contract_Regular.asp
International Society for Performance Improvement Job Bank	www.ispi.org
Jobs4HR.com	www.jobs4hr.com
HRlists.com	www.hrlists.com
Layoffjobs.com	www.layoffjobs.com
Media Human Resource Association	www.shrm.org/mhra/index.asp
NationJob Network: Human Resources Job Page	www.nationjob.com/hr
National Association of Colleges & Employers (NACE)	www.nacelink.com
National Council on Compensation Insurance Careers	www.ncci.com/ncciweb/ncci.asp?lf=control_panel.asp&mf=/ncciresearch/careers/careers.htm
Navigator Online	www.lwhra.org
Net Expat	www.netexpat.com
New Jersey Human Resource Planning Group	www.njhrpg.org
Northeast Human Resource Association Career Center	www.nehra.com/career.php?PHPSESSID=3370132aae438e135227dc62b488025c
OD Network On-line	www.odnetwork.org
Ohio State Council (SHRM)	www.ohioshrm.org
Personnel Management Association of Western New England	www.pmawne.org
The Portland Human Resource Management Association, Inc.	www.pdxnhrmashrm.org
Positive Employee Relations Council Network Job Opps	www.perc.net/hr.html
Professionals in Human Resource Association Career Center	www.pihra.org/capirasn/careers.nsf/home?open
RecruiterSeek	www.recruiterseek.com
SHRM Atlanta	www.shrmatlanta.org
SHRM Jacksonville	www.shrmjax.org
✵ Society for Human Resource Management HRJobs	www.shrm.org/jobs
TCM.com's HR Careers	www.tcm.com/hr-careers

Notes
Favorite sites, useful resources

Human Resources (continued)

Training Forum	www.trainingforum.com
Trainingjob.com	www.trainingjob.com
The Training SuperSite	www.trainingsupersite.com
Tri-State Human Resource Management Association	www.tri-state-hr.org
Tulsa Area Human Resources Association	www.tahra.org
WillTrainJobs.com	www.willtrainjobs.com
Workforce Online	www.workforceonline.com
World at Work Job Links [American Compensation Association]	www.worldatwork.org

-I-

Industrial/Manufacturing

Association of Industrial Metalizers, Coaters & Laminators	www.aimcal.org
Auto Glass Magazine	www.glass.org
CastingJobs.com	www.castingjobs.com
COBRA	www.nebulae.net/cobra/career.htm
Drilling Research Institute	www.drillers.com
Epro.com	www.epro.com
Finishing.com	www.finishing.com
FM Link-Facilities Management	www.fmlink.com
iHireManufacturingEngineers.com	www.ihiremanufacturingengineers.com
Iron & Steel Society	www.issource.org
Jobwerx	www.jobwerx.com
ManufacturingJob.com	www.manufacturingjob.com
Manufacturing Job Site	www.manufacturingjobsite.com
Manufacturing Job Store	www.manufacturingjobstore.com
ManufacturingJobs.com	www.manufacturingjobs.com
MDL CareerCenter	http://careercenter.devicelink.com
National Association of Industrial Technology	www.nait.org
Network Glass Jobs	www.glassjobs.net
OilCareer.com	www.oilcareer.com
The Oil Directory	www.oildirectory.com
Petroleum Services Association of Canada Employment	www.psac.ca
Power Builder Journal	http://sys-con.com/pbdj
Semicon	www.semicon.com
Semicon Bay	www.semiconbay.com

Notes
Favorite sites, useful resources

Industrial/Manufacturing (continued)

Sheet Metal and Air Conditioning
  Contractor's Association   www.smacna.org
Society of Petrologists & Well Log Analysts
  Job Opportunities   www.spwla.org
Subseaexplorer   www.subseaexplorer.com

Information Technology/Information Systems
Software, Hardware, Middleware, Client server, Web specialists

General

15 Seconds Job Classifieds	www.15seconds.com/
A1A Computer Jobs Mailing List	www.a1acomputerpros.net
A-Z Internet Jobs	www.a-zjobs.com
Ace thee Interview	www.acetheinterview.com
The Ada Project	www.cs.yale.edu/HTML/YALE/CS/HyPlans/tap/tap.html
AD&A Software Jobs Home Page	www.softwarejobs.com
The Advanced Computing Systems Association	http://usenix.org
Advisor Zone	www.advisorzone.com
AS400 Network	www.news400.com
Association for Computing Machinery Career Resource Center	http://career.acm.org/crc
Association for Educational Communications and Technology Job Center	www.aect.org
Association of Internet Professionals National Job Board	www.association.org
Association of Legal Information Systems Managers Job Listings	www.alism.org/jobs.htm
Asynchrony	www.asynchrony.com
Avatar Magazine	www.avatarmag.com
Beeline.com	www.beeline.com
Brain Buzz	www.brainbuzz.com
Brain Power	www.brainpower.com
CanadaIT.com	www.canadait.com
Canada Job	www.canadajob.com
CardBrowser.com	www.cardbrowser.com
CareerFile	www.careerfile.com
Career Magic	www.careermagic.com
Career Marketplace Network	www.careermarketplace.com
Career Shop	www.careershop.com
Cert Review	www.itspecialist.com
CIO.com	www.cio.com
CM Today (Configuration Management)	www.cmtoday.com/forums/career/index.cfm

Notes
Favorite sites, useful resources

Information Technology/Information Systems (continued)

General (continued)

CNET's Ultimate ISP Guide	www.cnet.com/content/reports/special/ISP/index.html
Cobol Jobs	www.coboljobs.com
Comforce	www.comforce.com
⛏ ComputerJobs.com	www.computerjobs.com
⛏ Computerwork.com	www.computerwork.com
Computing Research Association Job Announcements	www.cra.org/jobs/main/cra.jobs.html
Contract Employment Weekly	www.ceweekly.com
CREN	www.computingresources.com
CRN	www.crn.com/sections/careers/career.asp
Cyberking Employment	www.cyberkingemployment.com
Data Masters	www.datamasters.com
Developers.Net	www.developers1.net
Devhead	www.zdnet.com/devhead
⛏ DICE	www.dice.com
Digital Cat's	http://human.jobcats.com
Digital City	http://home.digitalcity.com/employment
Discover Jobs	www.discoverjobs.com
Dr. Dobb's	www.ddj.com
Domino Pro	www.dominopro.com
E-Cruiter	www.ecruiter.com
Eclectic [Netherlands]	www.eclectic.nl
eContent	www.ecmag.net
Educause	www.educause.edu
EE Times	www.eet.com
Elance	www.elance.com
Embedded.com	www.embedded.com
Emergit	www.emergit.com
eMoonlighter	www.emoonlighter.com
The Engineering Technology Site [United Kingdom]	www.engineers4engineers.co.uk
e-itwizards.com	www.e-itwizards.com
ePro.com	www.epro.com
eWork Exchange	www.ework.com
FatJob.com	www.fatjob.com
Free Agent	www.freeagent.com
GAAP Jobs	www.gaapjobs.com
H1B Sponsors	www.h1bsponsors.com
Hands on Solutions	www.handsonsolutions.com
Hardware-Jobs	www.hardware-jobs.net
Hi-Tech Careers	www.careermarthi-tech.com

Notes
Favorite sites, useful resources

Information Technology/Information Systems (continued)
General (continued)

Hi-Tech Club	www.hitechclub.com
Hightech-Jobs	www.high-tech-Jobs.net
High Technology Careers	www.hightechcareers.com
Hire Ability	www.hireability.com
Hot Dispatch	www.hotdispatch.com
Humanys.com	www.humanys.com
Huntahead	www.huntahead.com
InfiNet	www.infi.net
InformationWeek Career	www.informationweek.com/career
Informant Communications Group, Inc.	www.informant.com/icgmags.asp
In the Middle [United Kingdom]	www.inthemiddle.co.uk
Information Professionals	www.bring.com
Informix Jobs	www.premierjobs.com
Intega Online [United Kingdom]	www.intega.co.uk
Inter City Oz	http://interoz.com
Internet.com	http://jobs.internet.com
iSmart People	www.ismartpeople.com
ITcareers.com	www.itcareers.com
IT Classifieds	www.itclassifieds.com
IT Firms	www.itfirms.com
IT Hideout	www.hideout.com
TheITJobBoard.com [United Kingdom]	www.theitjobboard.com
IT Job Scooter	www.itjobscooter.com
IT Jobs in the United States	www.internet-solutions.com/itjobs/us/usselect.htm
IT Jobs Online	www.itjobsonline.com
ITonlinejobs.com	www.itonlinejobs.com
IT Solutions 2000	www.itsolutions2000.com
IT Talent	www.ittalent.com
IT webForum	www.it-webforum.com
ITCV [United Kingdom]	www.itcv.co.uk
JV Soaroh	www.jvsearch.com
Job Ads	www.jobads.com
Job Authority	www.jobauthority.com
JobCircle.com	www.jobcircle.com
Job Domain [United Kingdom]	www.jobdomain.co.uk
JobEngine	www.jobengine.com
The JobFactory	www.jobfactory.com
Job Island	www.jobisland.com
Job Net America	www.jobnetamerica.com
Job Serve	www.jobserve.com
JobUniverse.com	www.jobuniverse.com
JobUniverse.de [Germany]	www.jobuniverse.de

Notes
Favorite sites, useful resources

Information Technology/Information Systems (continued)

General (continued)

JobWarehouse.com	www.jobwarehouse.com
Job Warriors	http://jobwarriors.com
Job Webs	www.jobwebs.com
Jobs4IT.com	www.jobs4it.com
JobsDB	www.jobsdbusa.com
Jobs-net	www.jobs-net.com
Jobs-Network	www.jobs-network.com
Just Tech Jobs	www.justtechjobs.com
KR Solutions [United Kingdom]	www.krsolutions.co.uk
Lan-Jobs	www.lan-jobs.net
Lotus Notes Jobs	www.lotusnotesjobs.com
Mojolin	www.mojolin.com
MoreGeeks.com	www.moregeeks.com
Neo Soft	www.neosoft.com
Nerdworkz	www.nerdworkz.com
Net Mechanic	www.netmechanic.com
OperationIT	www.operationIT.com
Oxygen [United Kingdom]	www.oxygenonline.co.uk
PC World	www.pcworld.com
People Bonus	www.peoplebonus.com
PeopleOnline [Brazil]	www.peopleonline.com
PeopleSoft-Resources.com	www.peoplesoft-resources.com
PLACEUM 2000	www.placeum.com
Professional Exchange	www.professional-exchange.com/indexie.htm
Real-Time Magazine [Belgium]	www.realtime-info.be/encyc/magazine/magazine.htm
Real-Time Engineering	www.realtime-engineering.com
Road Whore	www.roadwhore.com
SAS Institute	www.sas.com/usergroups
Securityportal.com	www.securityportal.com
Semiconductor Jobs	www.semiconductorjobs.net
Skills Village	www.skillsvillage.com
Smarter Work	www.smarterwork.com
Soft Moonlighter	www.softmoonlightor.com
Software-Jobs	www.software-jobs.net
Society of Computer Professionals Online	www.comprof.com
Southern California Electronic Data Interchange Roundtable	www.scedir.org/html/jobs.html
Swift Jobs	www.swiftjobs.com
Tech-Engine	www.tech-engine.com
Tech Expo USA	www.techexpousa.com
TechEmployment.com	www.techemployment.com
Techie Gold	www.techiegold.com

Notes
Favorite sites, useful resources

WEDDLE's Helping to Maximize Your ROI ... Your Return on the Internet

Information Technology/Information Systems (continued)

General (continued)

techies.com	www.techies.com
Tech Job Bank	www.techjobbank.com
TechJobs	www.tech-jobs.net
TechResults	www.techresults.com
Tech Target	www.techtarget.com
TechWeb	www.techweb.com
Technology Jobs	www.technology-jobs.net
Techs	www.techs.com
VAR Business	www.channelweb.com/sections/careers/jobboard.asp
Virtual Job Fair	www.careerexpo.com
Wireless Developers	www.wirelessdevnet.com
Work Exchange	www.workexchange.com
Element K Journals	www.elementkjournals.com

AS400

Just AS/400 Jobs	www.justas400jobs.com
News400.com	www.news400.com

Baan

The Baan Fan Club	www.baanfans.com
Just BAAN Jobs	www.justbaanjobs.com

C++

C++ Jobs	www.cplusplusjobs.com
C++ Report	www.creport.com
C++ Users Group Job Links	www.hal9k.com/cug/jobs.htm
C Plus Plus Jobs	www.cplusplusjobs.com
Just C Jobs	www.justcjobs.com

Cobol

The Cobol Center	www.infogoal.com/cbd/cbdjob.htm
Just Cobol Jobs	www.justcoboljobs.com
Matt's Perfect COBOL Employment World	http://members.home.net/doormatt/jobs.html

Cold Fusion

Atlanta Cold Fusion	www.acfuq.org
Austin Cold Fusion	http://cftexas.outer.net/jobs.cfm
CF Programmers	www.cfprogrammers.com
Chicago Area Cold Fusion	www.chicfuq.org/jobs
Cold Fusion Advisor	www.cfadvisor.com
ColdFusion Support Conference	http://forums.allaire.com/devconf

Notes
Favorite sites, useful resources

WEDDLE's Helping to Maximize Your ROI ... Your Return on the Internet

Information Technology/Information Systems (continued)

Cold Fusion (continued)
House of Fusion   www.houseoffusion.com
Just Cold Fusion Jobs   www.justcoldfusionjobs.com
New England Allaire Developers   www.cfuqboston.com/index.cfm
New Jersey Cold Fusion   www.njcfq.org/njlive/default.com

Database
Database Analyst   www.databaseanalyst.com
Database Jobs   www.databasejobs.com
DBA Support   http://ora.dbasupport.com
Learn ASP   www.learnasp.com
International DB2 Users Group   www.idug.org
Just DB2 Jobs   www.justdb2jobs.com
LazyDBA.com   www.lazydba.com

Delphi
Delphi Jobs   www.delphijobs.com
Just Delphi Jobs   www.delphijobs.com

Electric Data Interchange
EDI Jobs Online   www.edijobsonline.com
EDI Coordinators & Consultants
  Clearinghouse   www.friend-edi.com
Just Exchange Jobs   www.justexchangejobs.com
Southern California Electronic Data
  Interchange Roundtable   www.scedir.org/html/jobs.html

ERP
ERP Assist   www.erpassist.com
ERP Central   www.erpcentral.com
ERP Fan Club   www.erpfans.com
ERP Jobs [Canada]   www.erp-jobs.com
ERP People   www.erp-people.com
ERP Professional   www.erpprofessional.com
ERP Software   www.erpsos.com
The ERP Supersite   www.tcchra.com

Java
All-Java-Jobs   www.all-java-jobs.com
City Java   www.cityjava.org
Digital Cat   http://human.javaresource.com
Java Jobs   www.javajobs.com/jobs.html
Java Jobs Online   www.javajobsonline.com
Java Programming Jobs and   http://java.superexpert.com/jobs/
  Java Programming Resumes   default.asp

Notes
Favorite sites, useful resources

Information Technology/Information Systems (continued)

Java (continued)
Java World	www.javaworld.com
jGuru	www.jguru.com
Just Java Jobs	www.justjavajobs.com
Team Java	www.teamjava.com

Lotus Notes
Association of ex-Lotus Employees	www.axle.org/careerframeset.html
Just Notes Jobs	www.justnotesjobs.com
Lavatech	www.lotusnotes.com
Lotus Notes Jobs	www.lotusnotesjobs.com

MacIntosh
MacTalent.com	www.mactalent.com
The Mac Trading Post	www.mymac2u.com/themactradingpost
MacWorld [United Kingdom]	www.macworld.co.uk/jobfinder
Macnologist	www.macnologist.com

Network/LAN/WAN
iHireNetworkAdministrators.com	www.ihirenetworkadministrators.com
Just Netware Jobs	www.justnetwarejobs.com
Just Networking Jobs	www.justnetworkingjobs.com
LAN Jobs	www.lanjobs.com
Network Engineer.com	www.networkengineer.com
Network World Fusion	www.nwfusion.com

Oracle
Just Oracle Jobs	www.justoraclejobs.com
Orafans.com	www.orafans.com
Oracle Contractor Database	www.cois.com/houg/con.html
Oracle Fan Club	www.oraclefans.com
Oracle Fans	www.oraclefans.com
Oracle Job Network	www.oracjobs.com
Oracle Jobs Network	www.orajobs.com/postjb1.htm
Oracle Professional	www.oracleprofessional.com
OraSearch	www.orasearch.com

PeopleSoft
Just People Soft Jobs	www.justpeoplesoftjobs.com
People Soft Fans	www.peoplesoftfans.com
People Soft Links	http://peoplesoftassist.com/peoplesoft_links.htm

Notes
Favorite sites, useful resources

WEDDLE's Helping to Maximize Your ROI ... Your Return on the Internet

Information Technology/Information Systems (continued)

Power Builder
Just Power Builder Jobs	www.justpowerbuilderjobs.com
Power Builder Jobs	www.powerbuilderjobs.com
Power Builder Journal	www.sys-con.com/pbdj/index2.html

Programming
iDevjobs.com	www.idevjobs.com
iHireProgrammers.com	wwwihireprogrammers.com
Jobs for Programmers	www.prgjobs.com
Programming-Webmaster	www.programming.com
Programming Jobs	www.programmingjobs.com
Programming-Services	www.programming-services.com
Superexpert	www.superexpert.com

SAP
A1A Computer Jobs Mailing List	www.a1acomputerpros.net
Just SAP Jobs	www.justsapjobs.com
SAP Club	www.sapclub.com
The SAP Fan Club	www.sapfans.com
SAPInfo.net	www.sapinfo.net
SAP Professional Organization	www.sap-professional.org
SAP Solutions	www.sap.com
The Spot 4 SAP	www.thespot4sap.com

Unix
Donohue's RS/6000 & UNIX Employment Site	www.s6000.com
Just UNIX Jobs	www.justunixjobs.com
Unix Guru Universe	www.ugu.com
Unix World	www.networkcomputing.com/unixworld/unixhome.html

Visual Basic
Just VB Jobs	www.justvbjobs.com
V Basic Search	www.vbasicsearch.com
VB Code Guru	http://codeguru.earthweb.com/vb
Visual Basic Jobs	www.visualbasicjobs.com

Web
B2B Frontline.com	www.b2bfrontline.com
CGI Resource Index	www.cgi-resources.com
HTML Writers Guild HWG-Jobs	www.hwg.org/lists/hwg-jobs
I-Advertising	http://internetadvertising.org
Just E-Commerce Jobs	www.juste-commercejobs.com

Notes
Favorite sites, useful resources

Information Technology/Information Systems (continued)

Web (continued)

Just Web Jobs	www.justwebjobs.com
Search Hound	www.searchhound.com
SGML/XML Jobs	www.eccnet.com/sgmluq/sgmljobs.html
Site Experts	www.siteexperts.com
US Internet Industry	www.usiia.org
Web Jobs USA	www.webjobsusa.com
Web Programming Jobs	www.webprogrammingjobs.com
Web Site Builder	www.websitebuilder.com
XMLephant	www.xmlephant.com

Windows

BHS Job Center	www.bhs.com/jobs2
Information NT	www.informationnt.com
Just NT Jobs	www.justntjobs.com
Just Windows Jobs	www.justwindowsjobs.com
NTPRO	www.ntpro.org/jobbank.html
Swynk.com	www.swynk.com
Windows NT Resource Center	www.bhs.com/default.asp

Other Specialty

American Statistical Association Statistics Career Center	www.amstat.org/careers
Association for Women in Computing	www.awc-hq.org
Black Data Processing Association Online	www.bdpa.org
Blackgeeks	www.blackgeeks.com
BroadbandCareers.com	www.broadbandcareers.com
Carolina Computer Jobs	www.carolinacomputerjobs.com
Common Switzerland	www.common.ch
Controller Jobs	www.controllerjobs.com
Donohue's RS/6000 & UNIX Employment Site	www.s6000.com
Ed Barlow's Sysbase Stuff	www.tiac.net/users/saltech
Electronic Media Online	www.emonline.com
Florida NACCB	www.floridanaccb.org
GISjobs.com	www.gisjobs.com
GIS Jobs Clearinghouse	www.gic.org
ITmoonlighter.com	www.itmoonlighter.com
Just Access Jobs	www.justaccessjobs.com
Just ASP Jobs	www.justaspjobs.com
Just Fox Pro Job	www.foxprojobs.com
Just Help Desk Jobs	www.justhelpdeskjobs.com
Just Informix Jobs	www.justinformixjobs.com
Just JD Edwards Jobs	www.justjdedwardsjobs.com
Just Mainframe Jobs	www.justmainframejobs.com

Notes
Favorite sites, useful resources

Information Technology/Information Systems (continued)
Other Specialty (continued)

Just OLAP Jobs	www.justolapjobs.com
Just Perl Jobs	www.justperljobs.com
Just Progress Jobs	www.justprogressjobs.com
Just Project Manager Jobs	www.justprogrammanagerjobs.com
Just Q A Jobs	www.justqajobs.com
Just Security Jobs	www.justsecurityjobs.com
Just Siebel Jobs	www.justsiebeljobs.com
Just SQL Server Jobs	www.justsqlserverjobs.com
Just Sybase Jobs	www.justsybasejobs.com
Just Tech Sales Jobs	www.justtechsalesjobs.com
Just Telephony Jobs	www.justelephonyjobs.com
Lapis Software	www.lapis.com
Midrange Computing Institute	www.midrangecomputing.com
MVShelp.com	www.mvshelp.com
NACCB - Dallas - Ft. Worth Chapter	www.dfw-naccb.org
Project Manager	www.projectmanager.com
See Beyond	www.seebeyond.com
Software Contractor's Guild	www.scguild.com
Software Developer	www.softwaredeveloper.com
Software Engineer	http://softwareengineer.comIn
Software & IT Sales Employment Review	www.salesrecruits.com
Software QA and Testing Resource Center	www.softwareqatest.com
Tech Writers	www.techwriters.com
Technical Communicator	www.technicalcommunicatior.com
University of Maryland Computer Science Grads	www.cs.umd.edu/users
Texas A&M University Computer Science Grads	www.cs.tamu.edu/Resumes
User Group News	www.ugn.com/index.html
Women in Information Technology	www.worldWIT.org
Women in Technology International (WITI) 4Hire	www.wIti4hire.com

Insurance

4 Insurance Jobs	www.4insurancejobs.com
Actuary.com	www.actuary.com
ActuaryJobs.com	www.actuaryjobs.com
American Institute for Chartered Property Casualty Underwriters	www.aicpcu.org
Chartered Property Casualty Underwriters	www.cpcusociety.org
Global Association of Risk Professionals Career Center	www.garp.com/careercenter/index.asp

Notes
Favorite sites, useful resources

Insurance (continued)

iHireInsurance.com	www.ihireinsurance.com
INSData	www.insdata.com
Insurance File	www.insfile.com
The Insurance Job Bank	www.iiin.com/html/jobs.html
InsuranceWorks.com [Canada]	www.insuranceworks.com
Life Career Retreat	www.lifecareer.com
LIMRA International	www.limra.com
National Council on Compensation Insurance Careers	www.ncci.com/ncciweb/ncci.asp?If=control_panel.asp&mf=/ncci research/careers/careers.htm
National Insurance Recruiters Association Online Job Database	www.nirassn.com/positions.cfm
NationJob Network: Financial, Accounting and Insurance Jobs Page	www.nationjob.com/financial
Property and Casualty	www.propertyandcasualty.com
Risk Info	www.riskinfo.com
Risk & Insurance Management Society Careers	www.rims.org/Template.cfm?Section=JobBank1&Template=/Jobbank/SearchJobForm.cfm
Ultimate Insurance Jobs	www.ultimateinsurancejobs.com
UnderwritingJobs.com	www.underwritingjobs.com

International

General

Anywhere You Go	www.anywhereyougo.com
Community Learning Network	www.cln.org
Empowered Network	http://empowerednetworks.com
Expat Exchange	www.expatexchange.com
Financial Job Network	www.financialjobnetwork.com
FT.com -Financial Times	www.ft.com
Global Health Network	http://info.pitt.edu/HOME/GHNet/GHNet.html
Global Workplace	www.global-workplace.com
Humanys.com	www.humanys.com
International Academic Job Market [Australia]	www.camrev.com.au/share/jobs.html
International Jobs Center	www.internationaljobs.org
International Personnel Management Association	www.ipma-hr.org
International Society for Molecular Plant-Microbe Interactions	www.ismpinet.org/career
International Union of Food	www.iuf.org
Jobs in Higher Education Geographical Listings	http://volvo.gslis.utexas.edu/~acadres/jobs/index.html

Notes
Favorite sites, useful resources

International (continued)
General (continued)
Jobs 4 All	www.jobs4all.com
Oil Online	www.oilonline.com
OneWorld.net	www.oneworld.org/jobs/index.html
OverseasJobsExpress	www.overseasjobs.com
Packinfo-World	www.packinfo-world.com
The Internet Pilot to Physics	http://physicsweb.org/TIPTOP
Sales & Marketing Executives International Career Center	www.smei.org/careers/index.shtml
Space Jobs	www.spacejobs.com
Top Jobs [United Kingdom]	www.topjobs.co.uk

Africa-General
Job Searching for Africa	www.sas.upenn.edu/African_Studies/Home_Page/menu_job_srch.html

Asia-General
Asia Inc.	www.asia-inc.com
Asia-Net	www.asia-net.com
Asia Wired	www.asiawired.com
Asiaco Jobs Center	http://jobs.asiaco.com
Asianpro.com	http://asianpro.com
CareerJournal Asia	www.careerjournalasia.com
Career Next	www.careernext.com
E4Asia	www.e4asia.com
Job Asia	www.jobasia.com
JobsDB	www.jobsdb.com
Job Street	www.jobstreet.com
Panda Career	www.pandacareer.com
Wang & Li Asia Resources Online	www.wang-li.com

Australia
Academia	http://academia.anu.edu.au/New
Ambition	www.ambition.com.au
The Australian Resume Server	www.herenow.com.au
CareerOne	www.careerone.com.au
Careers On Line	www.careersonline.com.au
Edonline.com.au	www.edonline.com.au
Employment Opportunities In Australia	www.employment.com.au
Fairfax Market	http://market.fairfax.com.au
International Academic Job Market	www.camrev.com.au/share/jobs.html
ITrecruitment.com.au	www.castle.com.au

Notes
Favorite sites, useful resources

International (continued)

Australia (continued)
Jobwire.com.au	www.jobwire.com.au
Learn SA	www.nexus.edu.au/learnsatext/default.htm
MyCareer.com.au	www.mycareer.com.au
Queensland Department of Primary Industries	www.dpi.qld.gov.au/cft
Ozland's Internet	http://cybermall.ozland.net.au/employ
SEEK	www.seek.com.au

Belgium
JobsCareer.be	www.jobs-career.be
Organic Chemistry Jobs Worldwide	www.organicworldwide.net/jobs/jobs.html

Bermuda
Bermuda Biological Station for Research, Inc.	www.bbsr.edu
BermudaJobs.com	www.bermudajobs.com

Brazil
PeopleOnline	www.peopleonline.com
Zeezo	http://brazil.zeezo.com/jobs.htm

Caribbean
CaribCareer.com	www.caribcareer.com
Caribbean JobFair	www.caribbeanjobfair.com
EscapeArtist	www.escapeartist.com
JobsintheSun.com	www.jobsinthesun.com
TropicJobs.com	www.tropicjobs.com

Canada
ACREQ	www.cre.qc.ca
ActiJob	www.actijob.com
Agricultural Employment in British Columbia	www.ioland.net/~awpb/emop/startag.html
Atlantic Canada Careers	www.brainstalent.com/careers_atlantic_canada.htm
BC Biotechnology Alliance	www.bcbiotech.ca
Brains Talent	www.brainstalent.com
CACEE Work Web	www.cacee.com/index.html
Calgary Job Shop	www.calgaryjobshop.ca
CanadaIT.com	www.canadait.com
Canada Job Search	www.canadajobsearch.com

Notes
Favorite sites, useful resources

International (continued)
Canada (continued)

Canada's Fifty-Plus	www.fifty-plus.net
Canadian Association of Career Educators & Employers	www.cacee.com
Canadian Careers	www.canadiancareers.com
Canadian Jobs Catalogue	www.kenevacorp.mb.ca
Canadian Relocation Systems	http://relocatecanada.com
Canadian Resume' Centre	www.canres.com
Canadian Society of Biochemistry and Mollecular and Cellular Biologists Experimental Medicine Job Listing	www.medcor.mcgill.ca/EXPMED/DOCS/jobs.html
Canadian Technical Recruiters Network	www.ctrn.com
Canjobs.com	www.canjobs.com
CanMed	www.canmed.com
CareerBridge	www.careerbridge.com
Careerclick.com	www.careerclick.com
Career Exchange	www.careerexchange.com
Career Internetworking	www.careerkey.com
Circuit Match	www.circuitmatch.com
Eastern Ontario Job Shop	www.easternontariojobshop.ca
Edmonton Job Shop	www.edmontonjobshop.ca
Electronic Labour Exchange	www.ele-spe.org
Employxpress	www.employxpress.com
Globe and Mail	www.theglobeandmail.com
Hcareers.com	www.hcareers.ca
Human Resource Professionals Association of Ontario	www.hrpao.org
InsuranceWorks.com	www.insuranceworks.com
Jobboom	www.jobboom.com
JobPostings.ca	www.jobpostings.ca
Job Shark	www.jobshark.com
Job Toaster	www.jobtoaster.com
Jobs Online Canada	www.jobsonline.ca
KW Job Shop	wwww.kwjobshop.ca
Lethbridge Job Shop	www.lethbridgejobshop.ca
MBA Network	www.mbanetwork.ca
Net @ccess	http://netaccess.on.ca
New Brunswick Job Shop	www.newbrunswickjobshop.ca
Newfoundland Labrador Job Shop	www.newfoundlandlabradorjobshop.ca
Nova Scotia Job Shop	www.novascotiajobshop.ca
Ottawa Area Computer Job Links Page	http://members.home.net/oacjlp
Ottawa Job Shop	www.ottawajobshop.ca
Payroll Jobs	www.payrolljobs.com
Petroleum Services Association of Canada	www.psac.ca

Notes
Favorite sites, useful resources

WEDDLE's Helping to Maximize Your ROI … Your Return on the Internet

International (continued)

Canada (continued)
RecruitersCafe.com	www.recruiterscafe.com
Regina Job Shop	www.reginajobshop.ca
Saskatoon Job Shop	www.saskatoonjobshop.ca
SCWIST Work Pathfinder	www.harbour.sfu.ca/scwist/pathfinder/index.htm
The Sixth Degree	www.thesixthdegree.com
Sympatico Work Place	http://workplace.sympatico.ca
TCM.com's HR Careers	www.tcm.com/hr-careers
Thompson Okanagan Job Shop	www.thompsonokanaganjobshop.ca
Toronto Job Shop	www.torontojobshop.ca
Toronto Jobs	www.toronto-jobs.com
Toronto Society of Financial Analysts	www.tsfa.ca
Tourism Work Web	www.tourismworkweb.com
Vancouver Job Shop	www.vancouverjobshop.ca
Vancouver Jobs	www.vancouver-jobs.com
Victoria Job Shop	www.victoriajobshop.ca
Winnipeg Job Shop	www.winnipegjobshop.ca
⚑ Workopolis	www.workopolis.com

Chile
ChileTech.com	www.chiletech.com
Zeezo	http://chile.zeezo.com/santiago-de-chile/jobs.htm

China
Asiaco Job Center	http://jobs.asiaco.com
AsiaOne Careers	www.asiaonecareers.com
CareerWise at Dragonsurf.com	www.dragonsurf.com/CareerWise/index.cfm
CC-Jobs.com	www.cc-jobs.com
BeijingJob.com	www.beijingjob.com
DragonSurf.com	www.dragonsurf.com
JobSquare	www.jobsquare.com
Zaobao	http://careers.zaobao.com
Zhaopin	www.zhaopin.com

Denmark
Job-Index	www.jobindex.dk
+ Jobs Danmark	www.denmark.plusjobs.com

Europe-General
AuPair In Europe	www.princeent.com/aupair
CareerJournal Europe	www.careerjournaleurope.com

Notes
Favorite sites, useful resources

International (continued)
Europe-General (continued)
CV-Online	www.cveurope.com
eFinancial Careers	www.efinancialcareers.com
Euroleaders	www.euroleaders.com
Jobline International	www.jobline.org
Job Pilot	www.jobpilot.com
Job Universe	www.jobuniverse.com
StepStone	www.stepstone.com
SupplyChainRecruit.com	www.supplychainrecruit.com
TipTopJob.com	www.tiptopjob.com
Wideyes	www.wideyes.co.uk

France
CEGOS Worldwide	www.cegos.fr
eFinancialCareers.fr	www.efinancialcareers.fr
JobPilot.fr	www.jobpilot.fr
Monster.fr	www.monster.fr

Guam
The Jobs Guam Job Search Site	www.post-a-job.com/allJobs/United_States/Guam/Guam.html
Job Search in Guam	www.worldtenant.com/jobs/guam.htm

Germany
Association for Applied Human Pharmacology	www.agah-web.de
City Jobs	www.cityjobs.com
E-JOE: European Job Opportunites for Economists	http://maynard.ww.tu-berlin.de/e-joe
EMBL Job Vacancies	www.embl-heidelberg.de/ExternalInfo/Jobs
Financial Times Deutschland	www.positionnet.de
Gormany USA	www.germany-usa.com
Jobline	www.jobline.de
JobLinks	http://cip.physik.uni-wuerzburg.de
Job Pilot	www.jobpilot.com
JobUniverse.de	www.jobuniverse.de
Worldwide Jobs	www.worldwidejobs.com

Hong Kong
CareerWise at Dragonsurf.com	www.dragonsurf.com/CareerWise/index.cfm
Hong Kong Jobs	www.hkjobs.com
Hong Kong Standard	www.hkstandard.com

Notes
Favorite sites, useful resources

WEDDLE's Helping to Maximize Your ROI ... Your Return on the Internet

International (continued)

India
Career India	www.careerindia.com
Career Mosaic India	www.careermosaicindia.com
Cyber India Online	www.ciol.com
HindJob.com	www.hindjob.com
Ikerala	www.ikerala.com
Jobs Ahead	www.jobsahead.com
Net Pilgrim	www.recruitmentindia.com
People.com	www.people.com
Win Jobs	www.winjobs.com

Ireland
Corporate Skills	www.irishjobs.com
Hcareers	www.hcareers.co.uk
Irishjobs	www.irishjobs.ie
The Irish Jobs Page	www.exp.ie
JobsinHealth	www.jobsinhealth.ie

Israel
Marksman	www.marksman.co.il
MyRecruiter.com	www.myrecruiter.com

Italy
JobOnline.it	www.jobonline.it
TalentManager	www.talentmanager.it

Japan
Career Forum	www.careerforum.net
Career Quest	www.venture-web.or.jp/axiom/axiom_english/index.html
Daijob.com	www.daijob.com
International Career Information, Inc.	www.rici.com
Japanese Jobs	www.japanesejobs.com
Job Easy	www.jobeasy.com
NAUKRI	www.naukri.com
O Hayo Sensei	www.ohayosensei.com/classified.html
Tokyo Classified	www.tokyoclassified.com
WorkinJapan	www.workinjapan.com

Korea
Asiaco Jobs Center	http://jobs.asiaco.com/southkorea/
Job Korea [not in English]	www.jobkorea.co.kr
Peoplenjob	www.peoplenjob.com

Notes
Favorite sites, useful resources

International (continued)

Latin America
Asiaco Jobs Center   http://jobs.asiaco.com/latinamerica/
Bumeran   www.bumeran.com
LatPro   www.latpro.com

Luxembourg
LuxJobs   www.luxjobs.lu
Monster.lu   www.monster.lu

Netherlands
City Jobs   www.cityjobs.com
EEGA   www.eega.nl
Hospitality Net Virtual Job Exchange www.hospitalitynet.nl
Jobs   www.jobs.nl
Van Zoelen Recruitment   www.vz-recruitment.nl/eng/indexen.htm

New Zealand
Executive Taskforce   http://exectask.co.nz
Nzjobs   www.nzjobs.co.nz

Peru
EC – Jobshark   www.ec-jobshark.com.pe
Zeezo   http://peru.zeezo.com/jobs.htm

Philippines
JobStreet Philippines   http://ph.jobstreet.com/
Jobs.NET   www.jobs.net
Philippines Employment Center   www.asiadragons.com/philippines/employment/
Philippines Jobs   http://philippinejobs.ph/

Scotland
Jobsword   www.jobsword.co.uk/scotland.html
ScotlandJobs.net   www.scotlandjobs.net
TechJobsScotland   www.techjobsscotland.com
WorkWithUs.org   www.workwithus.org/people/

Singapore
JobStreet.com   www.jobstreet.com
9to5Asia.com   www.9to5asia.com
Singapore and Asean Job Resume Database www.siam.net/jobs

Notes
Favorite sites, useful resources

International (continued)

Singapore (continued)
Singapore Jobs Directory	www.jobs.com.sg
SingaporeJobsOnline.com	www.singaporejobsonline.com

Spain
Monster Espania	www.monster.es
Sapnish-Living.com	www.spanish-living.com/index_links/jobs/jobs.html
Zeezo	http://spain.zeezo.com/jobs.htm

South Africa
Best Jobs South Africa	www.bestjobsza.com/dr-job.htm
CareerClassifieds South Africa	www.careerclassifieds.co.za/
Jobs.co.za	www.jobs.co.za

Switzerland
Common Switzerland	www.common.ch
Jobs-in-Europe.net	www.jobs-in-europe.net/swiss.html
Math-Jobs.ch	www.math-jobs.ch

Taiwan
CareerWise at Dragonsurf.com	www.dragonsurf.com/CareerWise/index.cfm
JobSlide.com	www.jobslide.com/directory/Country/Taiwan/

United Kingdom
1st Job	www.1stjob.co.uk
1st 4 UK HR Jobs	www.1st4ukhrjobs.co.uk
4 Weeks	www.4weeks.com
AccountingWeb	www.accountingweb.co.uk
Association of Clinical Research in the Pharmaceutical Industry	www.acrpi.com
Association of Graduate Careers Advisory Service [United Kingdom]	www.agcas.org.uk
Association of Online Recruiters	www.rec.uk.com
Aston University	www.aston.ac.uk
Bconstructive	www.bconstructive.co.uk
BigBlueDog.com	www.bigbluedog.com
Bookatemp.co.uk	www.bookatemp.co.uk
BUBL Employment Bulletin Board	http://bubl.ac.uk
Business Web Directory	www.businessdirectory.com
Call Centres	www.searchcallcentre.co.uk
CancerJobs.net	www.cancerjobs.net

Notes
Favorite sites, useful resources

International (continued)

United Kingdom (continued)

Career-Ahead	www.career-ahead.co.uk
CareersInRecruitment.com	www.careersinrecruitment.com
Change Jobs	www.changejobs.co.uk
Citifocus	www.citifocus.co.uk
CityJobs	www.citijobs.co.uk
Commserve	www.commserve.co.uk
Computer Staff	www.computerstaff.net
Confidential IT	www.confidentialit.com
Consultants on the Net	www.consultantsonthenet.com
The CV Index Directory	www.cvindex.com
CVServices.net	www.cvspecial.co.uk
Cyberia	www.cyberiacafe.net/jobs
CyberKing Employment	www.cyberkingemployment.com
CYMRU Prosper Wales	http://prosper.swan.ac.uk
Datascope Recruitment	www.datascope.co.uk
DERWeb	www.derweb.co.uk
DHA Resourcing Solutions	www.d-h-a.net
Discover Me	www.discoverme.com
Do-It	www.do-it.org.uk
Dot Jobs	www.dotjobs.co.uk
dotJournalism	www.journalism.co.uk
Easyline.co.uk	www.easyline.co.uk
Edie's Environmental Job Centre	www.edie.net
Eteach.com	www.eteach.com
Education-Jobs	www.education-jobs.co.uk
EFL Web	www.eflweb.com
e-job	www.e-job.net
Employment Postions Abroad	www.ecaltd.com/default.asp
ENDS	www.endsco.uk/jobs
The Engineering Technology Site	www.engineers4engineers.co.uk
Eplace.co.uk	www.eplace.co.uk
Escape Artist	www.escapeartist.com
Euro London	www.eurolondon.com
Execs on the Net	www.eotn.co.uk
ExecutiveOpenings.com	www.executiveopenings.com
ExecutivesontheWeb.com	www.executivesontheweb.com
First Choice Recruitment	www.first-choice-uk.co.uk
Fish4IT	www.fish4it.co.uk
Fish4Jobs	http://jobs.fish4.co.uk
Fledglings	www.fledglings.net
Freelawyer	www.freelawyer.coluk
Free-Recruitment.com	www.free-recruitment.com
G2legal	www.g2legal.co.uk
GAAPWeb.com	www.gaapweb.com

Notes
Favorite sites, useful resources

International (continued)

United Kingdom (continued)

GetHeadHunted	www.getheadhunted.co.uk
Go Partnership Limited	www.gogogo.org
The Guardian Observer	http://recruitnet.guardian.co.uk
Gisajob	www.gisajob.com
Go Job Site	www.gojobsite.com
Goldensquare.com	www.goldensquare.com
Graduate-jobs.com	www.graduate-jobs.com
GraduateLink	www.graduatelink.com
Gradunet	www.gradunet.co.uk
Grapevine Jobs	www.grapevinejobs.com
GTNews	www.gtnews.com
Hands on Solutions	www.handsonsolutions.com
Hcareers	www.hcareers.co.uk
Hotcourses.com	www.givemeajob.co.uk
Hot Recruit	www.hotrecruit.co.uk
Hotel Jobs	www.hotel-jobs.co.uk
HR Staff	www.hrstaff.co.uk
Hy-phen	www.hy-phen.com
Gradvacs.com	www.gradvacs.com
In the Middle	www.inthemiddle.co.uk
The Independent Consultants Network	www.inconet.com
InHR	www.inhr.co.uk
InRetail	www.inretail.co.uk
Intega Online	www.intega.co.uk
I-Resign.co	www.i-resign.com/uk/home/default.asp
TheITJobBoard.com	www.theitjobboard.com
IT List	www.itlist.co.uk
It's A People Thing!	www.itsapeoplething.com
ITCV	www.itcv.co.uk
Jim Finder	www.jimfinder.com
Jobs4a.com	www.jobs4a.com
Job4me.com	wwwjob4me.com
Jobcorner	www.jobcorner.com
JobChannel	www.jobchannol.tv
Job Domain	www.jobdomain.co.uk
Job Finder	www.jobfinder.com
Job Force	www.jobforce.com
Job Jobbed	www.jobjobbed.com
Job Magic	www.jobmagic.net
Job Magnet	www.jobmagnet.co.uk
Job-opps.co.uk	www.job-opps-co.uk
JobPilot UK	www.jobpilot.co.uk
JobScout	www.jobscout.co.uk

Notes
Favorite sites, useful resources

International (continued)

United Kingdom (continued)

Job Search UK	www.jobsearch.co.uk
Job Serve	www.jobserve.com
Jobshark.com	www.jobshark.co.uk
Job Shop	www.workweb.co.uk
JobSite UK	www.jobsite.co.uk
Job-surf.com	www.job-surf.com
JobTrack Online	www.jobtrack.co.uk
Job Watch	www.jobwatch.co.uk
Jobworld UK	www.jobworld.oc.uk
jobbies.com	www.jobbies.com
Jobs.ac.uk	www.jobs.ac.uk
Jobs-at	www.jobs-at.co.uk
Jobs.co.uk	www.jobs.co.uk
Jobsandadverts.com	www.jobsandadverts.com
Jobsgopublic	www.jobsgopublic.co.uk
Jobsin.co.uk	www.jobsin.co.uk
Jobs in Marketing	www.jobs-in-marketing.co.uk
Jobs Jobs Jobs	www.jobsjobsjobs.co.uk
Jobs.telegraph.co.uk	www.appointments-plus.com
Jobs Unlimited	www.jobsunlimited.co.uk
JobsWithBalls.com	www.jobswithballs.com
Johnston Vere	www.johnstonvere.com
Just Engineers	www.justengineers.net
Just Go Contract!	www.gocontract.com
Just Graduates	www.justgraduates.net
KR Solutions	www.krsolutions.co.uk
Laser Computer Recruitment	www.laserrec.co.uk
Leisure Opportunities	www.leisureopportunities.co.uk
Local Government Jobs	www.lgjobs.com
Locum Group Recruitment	www.locumgroup.co.uk
London Careers	www.londoncareers.net
London Jobs	www.londonjobs.co.uk
Mandy.com	www.mandy.com
Marine Recruitment Co.	www.marine-recruitment.co.uk
MedicSolve.com	www.medicsolve.com
Medjobsuk.com	www.medjobsuk.com
MightyMatch.com	www.mightymatch.com
Milkround Online	www.milkround.co.uk
Monster.com UK	www.monster.co.uk
Mycvonline UK	www.mycvonline.co.uk
My Oyster	www.myoyster.com
National Information Services and Systems	www.niss.ac.uk/noticeboard/index.html
Net J	www.netjobs.co.uk

Notes
Favorite sites, useful resources

International (continued)
United Kingdom (continued)

NewMonday.co.uk	www.newmonday.co.uk
Nixers.com	www.nixers.com
NMC4Jobs.com	www.nmc4jobs.com
Northwest Workplace	www.northwestworkplace.com
Nurseserve	www.nurseserv.co.uk
Oil Careers	www.oilcareers.com
Online Context UK	www.onlinecontentuk.org
Phee Farrer Jones Consultancy	www.pheefarrerjones.co.uk
PhoneAJob	www.phoneajob.com
Planet Recruit	www.planetrecruit.co.uk
PTO People	www.ptopeople.co.uk
OutdoorStaff	www.outdoorstaff.co.uk
Oxygen	www.oxygenonline.co.uk
Qworx.com	www.qworx.com
Recruit PLC	www.newdawn.co.uk/recruit
Recruitment-Consultant.com	www.recruitment-consultant.com
Recruitment Jobz	www.recruitmentjobz.com
Resourcing International Consulting	www.cyber-cv.com
Resortjobs.co.uk	www.resortjobs.co.uk
Retail Moves	www.retailmoves.com
Searching the Universe	www.oconnell.co.uk
Smarter Work	www.smarterwork.com
SmugOne.com	www.smugone.com
StepStone	www.stepstone.co.uk
THESIS: The Times Higher Education Supplement InterView Service	www.thesis.co.uk
Talent Manager	www.talentmanager.com
Tandem-World.com	www.tandem-world.com
TAPS	http://taps.com
Temps Online	www.tempsonline.co.uk
Tempz	www.tempz.com
ThisIsJobs	www.thisisjobs.co.uk
Top Contracts	www.topcontacts.com
Top Jobs	www.topjobs.net
Top Jobs On the Net	www.topjobs.co.uk
Total Jobs	www.totaljobs.com
UK Graduate Careers	www.gti.co.uk
UKjobs2004.com	www.ukjobs2004.com
UK Vacancy Boards	www.nmib.com/course/vacboard.htm
Workthing.com	www.workthing.com

Venezuela

MeQuieroIr.com	www.mequieroir.com

Notes
Favorite sites, useful resources

Investment/Brokerage

BrokerHunter.com	www.brokerhunter.com
National Association of Securities Professionals Current Openings	www.nasphq.com/career.html
National Association of Securities Professionals (Atlanta) Current Openings	www.naspatlanta.com/career.html
National Association of Securities Professionals (New York) Underground Railroad	www.nasp-ny.org

-J-

Job Fairs Online

Job Dex	www.jobdex.com
OilCareerFair	www.oilcareerfair.com
Professional Exchange	www.professional-exchange.com/indexie.htm

Journalism & Media (see also Graphic Arts)

Airwaves Job Services	www.airwaves.com
Association of Electronic Journalists	www.rtnda.org
Association for Women in Communications	www.womcom.org
Association for Women in Communcations WDC Chapter	www.awic-dc.org
Communications Roundtable	www.roundtable.org
Copy Editor	www.copyeditor.com/jobsoverview.html
Copy Editor Newsletter	www.copyeditorjobs.com
Coroflot	www.coroflot.com
Creative Freelancers	www.freelnacers.com
dotJournalism [United Kingdom]	www.journalism.co.uk
Editor & Publisher	www.mediainfo.com
eFront.com	www.efront.com
Electronic Media Online	www.emonline.com
HTML Writers Guild HWG-Jobs	www.hwg.org/lists/hwg-jobs
I-Advertising	http://internetadvertising.org
International Association of Business Communicators Career Centre	www.iabc.com
JobLink for Journalists	http://ajr.newslink.org/joblink.html
JournalismJob.com	www.journalismjob.com
Journalism Jobs	www.journalismjobs.com
Mandy.com	www.mandy.com/1/filmtvjobs.ctm
Mediabistro	www.mediabistro.com
Media Communications Association International Job Hotline	www.itva.org/resources/job_hotline.htm

Notes
Favorite sites, useful resources

Journalism & Media (continued)

Media Human Resource Association	www.shrm.org/mhra/index.asp
Medialine	www.medialine.com
MediaRecruiter.com	www.mediarecruiter.com
National Diversity Newspaper Job Bank	www.newsjobs.com
National Writers Union Job Hotline	www.nwu.org/hotline
NationJob Advertising and Media Jobs Page	www.nationjob.com/media
New York New Media Association	www.nynma.org
News Jobs	www.newsjobs.com
Print Jobs	www.printjobs.com
R & R Online	www.rronline.com
Radio Ink Help Wanted	www.radioinkhelpwanted.com
Silicon Alley Connections	www.salley.com
Society for Technical Communications	www.stc.org
StaffWriters Plus, Inc.	www.staffwriters.com
Technical Communicator	www.technicalcommunicatior.com
TV Jobs	www.tvjobs.com
Ultimate TV	www.ultimatetv.com
Webmonkey Jobs	www.hotwired.com/dreamjobs
Workinpr.com	www.workinpr.com
The Write Jobs	www.writerswrite.com/jobs
The Write Jobs for The Writers Write	www.writerswrite.com/jobs
Writer's SunOasis	www.sunoasis.com

-L-

Law

4 Paralegals	www.4paralegals.com
AACN Career Opportunites	www.acca.com/jobline
American Association of Law Libraries Job Placement Hotline	www.aallnet.org/hotline
American Bar Association	www.abanet.org
American Corporate Counsel Association	www.acca.com
American Immmigration Lawyers Association	www.aila.org
Association of Legal Information Systems Managers Job Listings	www.alism.org/jobs.htm
Attorney Jobs	www.attorneyjobs.com
Attorney Pages	http://adviceco3.webex.net
Barry University of Orlando	www.uo.edu
Bench & Bar	www.mnbar.org/bbclass.htm
Counsel.net	www.counel.net
Degree Hunter	www.degreehunter.com

Notes
Favorite sites, useful resources

Law (continued)

Elite Consultants	www.eliteconsultants.com
Emplawyernet	www.emplawyernet.com
Find Law Careers	www.findlaw.com
Find Law Job	www.findlawjob.com
G2legal [United Kingdom]	www.g2legal.co.uk
Greedy Associates	www.greedyassociates.com
Hieros Gamos Legal Employment Classified	www.cgsg.com/hg/employ.html
iHireLegal	www.ihirelegal.com
Infirmation	www.infirmation.com
Intelproplaw	www.intelproplaw.com
The International Lawyers Network	www.lawinternational.com
JobLinks for Lawyers	htttp://home.sprynet.com/~ear2ground
JobsLawInfo.com	http://jobs.lawinfo.com
Law.com	www.law.com
Law Bulletin	www.lawbulletin.com
Law Forum	www.lawforum.net
Law Guru	www.lawguru.com
Law Info	www.lawinfo.com
Law Jobs	www.lawjobs.com
Law Match	http://lawmatch.com
Law Office	www.lawoffice.com
Law Source	http://lawsource.com
Lawyers – About.com	http://lawyers.about.com
Lawyers Weekly Jobs	www.lawyersweeklyjobs.com
⌘ The Legal Career Center Network	www.thelccn.com
The Legal Employment Search Site	www.legalemploy.com
Legal Gate	www.legalgate.com
Legal Hire	www.legalhire.com
Legal Job Store	www.legaljobstore.com
Legal Report	www.legalreport.com
Legal Search Network	wwwlegalsearchnetwork.com
Legal Serve	www.legalserve.com
Legal Staff	www.legalstaff.com
National Association of Legal Assistants	www.nala.org
National Employment Lawyers Association	www.nela.org
National Federation of Paralegal Associations Career Center	www.paralegals.org/Center/home.html
National Paralegal	www.nationalparalegal.org
New Hampshire Legal Assistance	www.nhla.org
Paralegal Classifieds	www.paralegalclassifieds.com
PatentJobs.com	www.patentjobs.com
Piper Pat	www.piperpat.co.nz
Trial Lawyers for Public Justice	www.tlpj.com

Notes
Favorite sites, useful resources

Law Enforcement

⚠ The Blue Line: Police Opportunity Monitor — www.theblueline.com
Cop Spot — www.cop-spot.com
High Technology Crime Investigation
  Association — www.htcia.org
iHireLawEnforcement.com — www.ihirelawenforcement.com
LawEnforcementJobs.com — www.lawenforcementjob.com

Library & Information Science

American Association of Law Libraries
  Job Placement Hotline — www.aallnet.org/hotline
American Library Association
  Library Education and Employment
  Menu Page — www.ala.org/education
Art Libraries Society of North America JobNet — http://arlisna.org/jobs.html
BUBL Employment Bulletin Board
  [United Kingdom] — http://bubl.ac.uk
Media Central — www.mediacentral.com/careers
Special Libraries Association — www.sla.org

Linguistics

Academic Job Openings in Applied Linguistics — http://aaaljobs.lang.uiuc.edu/
Jobs in Linguistics — www.linguistlist.org/jobsindex.html
Linguistic Enterprises — http://web.gc.cuny.edu/dept/lingu/enter/
The Linguist List — http://linguistlist.org/jobs/index.html

Logistics

FM Link-Facilities Management — www.fmlink.com
Jobstor.com — www.jobstor.com
JobsInLogistics.com — www.jobsinlogistics.com
LogisticsJobShop.com [United Kingdom] — www.logisticsjobshop.com
Logistics World — www.logisticsworld.com
MaintenanceEmployment.com — www.maintenanceemployment.com
RoadWhore.com — www.roadwhore.com
SupplyChainRecruit.com [Europe] — www.supplychainrecruit.com
Truckdriver.com — www.truckdriver.com
Virtual Logistics Directory — www.logisticsdirectory.com

Find Great Talent. ☛ WEDDLE's 2004 Recruiter's Guide

Notes
Favorite sites, useful resources

-M-

Military Personnel Transitioning into the Private Sector

Army Career & Alumni Program	www.acap.army.mil
Blue-to-Gray	www.bluetogray.com
Center for Employment Management	www.cemjob.com
Classified Employment Web-Site	www.yourinfosource.com/ CLEWS
ClearanceJobs.com	www.clearancejobs.com
Connecting Corporations to the Military Community	www.vets4hire.com
Corporate Gray Online	www.corporategrayonline.com
Green-to-Gray	www.greentogray.com
Hire Quality	www.hire-quality.com
Operation Transition	www.dmdc.osd.mil/ot
Military.com	www.military.com
Military Careers	www.militarycareers.com
Military Connections	www.militaryconnections.com
MilitaryHire.com	www.militaryhire.com
Mil2civ.com	www.mil2civ.com
Military Spouses	www.militaryspouses.com
My Future	www.myfuture.com
RecruitMarines.com	www.recruitmarines.com
RecruitMilitary.com	www.recruitmilitary.com
RecruitNavy.com	www.recruitnavy.com
Reserve Officers Association	www.roa.org/career_center.asp
Transition Assistance Online	www.taonline.com
★ VetJobs.com	www.vetjobs.com
Vets of Color	www.vetsofcolor.com

Modeling

ModelService.com	www.modelservice.com
OneModelPlace.com	www.onemodelplace.com
Supermodel.com	www.supermodel.com

Music

FilmMusic.net	www.filmmusic.net/ currentjobs.pdf
The Internet Music Pages	www.musicpages.com
Key Signature [United Kingdom]	www.keysignature.co.uk
MusicJObsOnline.net	www.musicjobsonline.net
MusiciansBuyLine.com	www.musiciansbuyline.com/ music_jobs_avail.html

Notes
Favorite sites, useful resources

WEDDLE's Helping to Maximize Your ROI ... Your Return on the Internet

-N-

Non-Profit

411 Fundraising	www.411fundraising.com
Career Action Center	www.careeraction.org
Chronicle of Philanthropy	www.philanthropy.com
Community Career Center	www.nonprofitjobs.org
The Foundation Center	www.fdncenter.org
Fundraising Jobs	www.fundraisingjobs.com
Good Works	www.essential.org
Idealist	www.idealist.org
Internet Nonprofit Center	www.nonprofits.org
International Service Agencies	www.charity.org
Localstaff.com	www.localstaff.com
The National Assembly	www.nassembly.org
Non Profit Career Network	www.nonprofitcareer.com
Nonprofit Charitable Organizations	www.nonprofit.about.com
Non Profit Employment	www.nonprofitemployment.com
Non-Profit Marketing	www.cob.ohio-state.edu/~fin/Nonprofit.htm
Opportunity Nocs	www.opnocsne.org
Philanthropy News Network Online	www.pnnonline.org/jobs
Social Service	www.socialservice.com
Tripod	www.tripod.com
VolunteerMatch	www.volunteermatch.org/

-O-

Outdoors/Recreation/Sports

C.O.A.C.H.	www.coachhelp.com
Coach's Nationwide Job Board	www.coachhelp.com/jobs.htm
Coaching Staff	www.coachingstaff.com
Cool Works	www.coolworks.com/showme
Cruise Job Link	www.cruisejoblink.com
Equimax	www.equimax.com
Great Summer Jobs	www.gsj.petersons.com
Horticultural Jobs	www.horticulturaljobs.com
Jobs In Sports	www.jobsinsports.com
JobsWithBalls.com [United Kingdom]	www.jobswithballs.com
Leisure Opportunities [United Kingdom]	www.leisureopportunities.co.uk
Lifeguarding Jobs	www.lifeguardingjobs.com
NascarCareers.com	www.nascarcareers.com
National Sports Employment News	www.sportsemployment.com
NCAA	www.ncaa.org/market/ads

Notes
Favorite sites, useful resources

Outdoors/Recreation/Sports (continued)

Northeast Athletic Job Link	www.bright.net/~joblink
Online Sports Career Center	www.onlinesports.com/careercenter.html
Outdoor Job Net	www.outdoornetwork.com/jobnetdb/default.html
OutdoorStaff [United Kingdom]	www.outdoorstaff.co.uk
Pet-Sitters.biz	www.pet-sitters.biz
PGA.com	www.pga.com
Resort Jobs	www.resortjobs.com
Resortjobs.co.uk [United Kingdom]	www.resortjobs.co.uk
Skiing the Net	www.skiingthenet.com
SportLink	www.sportlink.com
Sportscasting Jobs	www.sportscastingjobs.com
SportsJobs.com	www.sportsjobs.com
SummerJobs.com	www.summerjobs.com
Tennis Jobs	www.tennisjobs.com
Travel Jobz	www.traveljobz.net

-P-

Packaging for Food & Drug

Association of Industrial Metalizers, Coaters & Laminators	www.aimcal.org
Composite Can & Tube Institute	www.cctiwdc.org
Foodservice.com	http://foodservice.com
Institute of Food Science & Technology	www.ifst.org
Supermarket News	www.supermarketnews.com
Technical Association of the Pulp & Paper Industry Jobline	www.tappi.org/index.asp?ip=-1&ch=14&rc=-1

Pharmaceutical

Academy of Managed Care Pharmacy	www.amcp.org
American Academy of Pharmaceutical Physicians	www.aapp.org
American Association of Pharmaceutical Scientists	www.aaps.pharmaceutica.com/careerCenter/job_listing.asp
American College of Clinical Pharmacology	www.accp1.org
American College of Clinical Pharmacy	www.accp.com
American Society of Clinical Pharmacology and Therapeutics	www.ascpt.org
American Society of Health-System Pharmacists	www.ashp.com
American Society of Pharmacognosy	www.phcog.org

Notes
Favorite sites, useful resources

Pharmaceutical (continued)

Association for Applied Human Pharmacology [Germany]	www.agah-web.de
Association of Clinical Research in the Pharmaceutical Industry [United Kingdom]	www.acrpi.com
The Biomedical Engineering Network	www.bmenet.org
Board of Pharmaceutical Specialties	www.bpsweb.org
Carefree Pharmaceutical Returns	http://members.aol.com/ajnovotny/cpr2.htm
Drug Discovery Online	www.drugdiscoveryonline.com
Drug Information Association Employment Opportunities	www.diahome.org/docs/Jobs/Jobs_index.cfm
Georgia Pharmacy Association	www.gpha.org
International Pharmajobs	www.pharmajobs.com
ISPE Online	www.ispe.org
JobPharmaceuticals.com	www.jobpharmaceuticals.com
JobPharmacist.com	www.jobpharmacist.com
JobPharmacy.com	www.jobpharmacy.com
JobMedicine.com	www.jobmedicine.com
Michigan Pharmacists Association	www.mipharm.com
Missouri Pharmacy Association	www.morx.com
National Association of Boards of Pharmacy	www.nabp.net
Pharmaceutical Job Site	www.pharmaceuticaljobsite.com
PharmaceuticalJobsUSA.com	www.pharmaceuticaljobsusa.com
PharmacyChoice.com	www.pharmacychoice.com
PharmacyWeek.com	www.pweek.com
Pharmasys	www.pharmweb.com
RPhrecruiter.com	www.rphrecruiter.com
Rx Career Center	www.rxcareercenter.com
Rx Immigration	www.rximmigration.com

Physics

American Institute of Physics Career Services	www.aip.org/industry.html
Board of Physics & Astronomy	www.nas.edu/bpa
Institute of Physics	www.iop.org
JobLinks [Germany]	http://cip.physik.uni-wuerzburg.de/Job/
Optics.org	http://optics.org/home.ssi
Physics Jobs Online	www.tp.umu.se/TIPTOP/FORUM/JOBS
Plasma Gate [Israel]	http://plasma-gate.weizmann.ac.il

**Looking for a new or better job? Looking for top talent?
Use WEDDLE's publications. See the Catalog in this book.**

Notes
Favorite sites, useful resources

Printing & Bookbinding

The Bookbinders Guild of New York Job Bank	www.bbgny.com/guild/jb.html
Digital Printing and Imaging Association Employment Exchange (with the Screenprinting & Graphic Imaging Association International)	www.sgia.org/ employ/employ.html
Graphic Artists Information Network	www.gain.org
National Association for Printing Leadership	www.napl.org
PressTemps	www.presstemps.com
Printing Impressions	www.piworld.com

Public Sector/Government

⊠ The Blue Line: Police Opportunity Monitor	www.theblueline.com
Centers for Disease Control	www.cdc.gov
Civil Jobs	www.civiljobs.com
Cop Spot	www.cop-spot.com
Defense Jobs	www.defensejobs.com
DEM Job	www.demjob.com
Fed World	www.fedworld.gov
Federal Job Search	www.federaljobsearch.com
Federal Jobs Digest	www.jobsfed.com
FRS	www.fedjobs.com
GetaGovJob.com	www.getagovjob.com
GOP Job	www.gopjob.com
Governmentjobs.com	www.governmentjobs.com
GovMedCareers.com	www.govmedcareers.com
High Technology Crime Investigation Association	www.htcia.org
Intelligence Careers	www.intelligencecareers.com
Internet Job Source	http://statejobs.com
Jobsgopublic [United Kingdom]	www.jobsgopublic.co.uk
Jobs In Government	www.jobsingovernment.com
Military.com	www.military.com
NASA Jobs	www.nasajobs.nasa.gov
NavyJobs.com	www.navyjobs.com
Poli Temps	www.politemps.com
Police Employment	www.policeemployment.com
Political Resources	http://politicalresources.com
Public Service Employees	www.pse-net.com
Security Jobs Network	www.securityjobs.net
United States Department of Labor	www.dol.gov
US Air Force Careers	www.af.mil/careers
U.S. Office of Personnel Management	www.usajobs.opm.gov

Notes
Favorite sites, useful resources

Publishing

American Journalism Review Online — www.newslink.org/joblink.html
The Bookbinders Guild of
  New York Job Bank — www.bbgny.com//guild/jb.html
Council of Literary Magazines & Presses — www.clmp.org/jobs/jobs.html
Fulfillment Management Association, Inc. — www.fmanational.org
National Writer's Union Job Hotline — www.nwu.org/hotline/index.com
PrioritySearch.com — www.prioritysearch.com

Purchasing

BuyingJobs.com — www.buyingjobs.com
Institute for Supply Management
  Career Center — www.ism.ws/CareerCenter/index.cfm
Manufacturing-Engineering-Jobs.com — www.manufacturing-engineering-jobs.com
SupplyChainRecruit.com — www.supplychainrecruit.com

-Q-

Quality/Quality Control

iHireQualityControl.com — www.ihirequalitycontrol.com
I Six Sigma — www.isixsigma.com
Just QA Jobs — www.justqajobs.com
QA-Jobs — www.qa-jobs.com
QCEmployMe.com — www.qcemployme.com
Quality America — www.qualityamerica.com
Quality Today [United Kingdom] — www.qualitytoday.co.uk
Software QA and Testing Resource Center — www.softwareqatest.com

-R-

Real Estate

American Real Estate Society — www.aresnet.org/ARES/jobs/currjobs.html
Apartment Careers — www.apartmentcareers.com
California Mortgage Brokers Association
  Career Center — www.cambweb.org
Commercial Real Estate Jobs — www.loopnet.com/asp/jobs/index.asp
Escrowboard.com — www.escrowboard.com
FacilitiesJobs.com — www.facilitiesjobs.com
iHireRealEstate.com — www.ihirerealestate.com

Notes
Favorite sites, useful resources

Real Estate (continued)

Institute of Real Estate Management Jobs Bulletin	www.irem.org/i06_ind_res/html/post.html
Job Directories	www.inrealty.com/rs/jobs.html
Jobsite.com	www.jobsite.com
Leasing Jobs	www.leasingjobs.com
Loan Closer Jobs	www.loancloserjobs.com
Loan Originator Jobs	www.loanoriginatorjobs.com
Loop Net	www.loopnet.com
MortgageBoard.com	www.mortgageboard.com
Mortgage Job Market	www.jobmag.com
Mortgage Jobstore	www.mortgagejobstore.com
NACORE International	www.nacore.com
National Network of Commercial Real Estate Women Job Bank	www.nncrew.org/job_bank/job_bank_introduction_frm.html
NewHomeSalesJobs.com	www.newhomesalesjobs.com
Pike Net	www.pikenet.com
Real Estate Best Jobs	www.realestatebestjobs.com
Real Estate Careers	www.restatecareer.com
Real Estate Finance Jobs	www.realestatefinancejobs.com
Real Estate Job Store	www.realestatejobstore.com
Real Jobs	www.real-jobs.com
Titleboard.com	www.titleboard.com

Recruiters Resources

AIRS Directory	www.airsdirectory.com
Alliance of Medical Recruiters	www.physicianrecruiters.com/amrapp.htm
American Staffing Association	www.staffingtoday.net
Arizona Technical Recruiters Association	http://atra.hypermart.net
Association of Executive Search Consultants	www.aesc.org
Association of Financial Search Consultants	www.afsc-jobs.com
Atlanta Human Resources Association	www.harb.net/ahra
BrainHunter	www.brainhunter.com
The Breckenridge Group, Inc.	www.breckenridgegroup.com
California Staffing Professionals	www.catss.org
Canadian Technical Recruiters Network	www.ctrn.org
Career Highway.com	www.careerhighway.com
CareerSite	www.careersite.com
Colorado Technical Recruiters Network	www.ctrn.org
CyberEdit	www.cyberedit.com
DataFrenzy.com	www.datafrenzy.com
Defense Outplacement Referral System	www.dmdc.osd.mil/dors
Delaware Valley Technical Recruiters Network	www.dvtrn.org
DFW Recruiters Network	www.dfwrecruiters.com

Notes
Favorite sites, useful resources

Recruiters Resources (continued)

Drake Beam Morin	www.dbm.com/dbm.html
Electronic Recruiters Exchange	www.erexchange.com
Employment Management Association	www.shrm.org/ema/index.html
eQuest	www.joblauncher.com
ExecutiveResumes.com	www.executiveresumes.com
Free-For-Recruiters	www.free-for-recruiters.com
Global Media	www.globalmediarecruitment.com
GotResumes.com	www.gotresumes.com
Houston High Tech Recruiters Network	www.hhtrn.org
Illinois Association of Personnel Services	www.searchfirm.com/organizations/iaps/iaps.asp
Interbiznet.com	www.interbiznet.com/hrstart.html
International Association of Corporate and Professional Recruitment	www.iacpr.org
Investment Positions	www.investmentpositions.com
Its Your Job Now	www.itsyourjobnow.com
Lead411.com	www.lead411.com
Lee Hecht Harrison	www.careerlhh.com
Metro Atlanta High Tech Personnel Association	http://mahtpa.hom.mindspring.com
Minnesota Technical Recruiters Network	www.mntrn.com
MovingCenter.com	www.movingcenter.com
National Association of Executive Recruiters	www.naer.org
National Association for Health Care Recruitment	www.nahcr.com
National Association of Legal Search Consultants	www.nalsc.org
National Association of Personnel Services	www.napsweb.org
National Association of Physician Recruiters	www.napr.org
National Insurance Recruiters Association Online Job Database	www.nirassn.com/positions.cfm
National Technical Staffing Association	www.ntsa.com
New Jersey Staffing Association	www.njsa.com
New Jersey Technical Recruiters Alliance	www.njtra.org
New York Technical Recruiters Association	www.nytra.com
Northeast Human Resource Association	www.nehra.org
Northwest Recruiters Association	www.nwrecruit.org
Personnel Management Association of Western New England	www.pmawne.org
PickaJob.com	www.pickajob.com
Pittsburgh Personnel Association	ww.ppapitt.org
The Portland Human Resource Management Association, Inc.	www.pdxnhrmashrm.org
Professionals in Human Resource Association Career Center	www.pihra.org/capirasn/careers.nsf/home?open

Notes
Favorite sites, useful resources

Recruiters Resources (continued)

Project S.A.M.E.	http://netrecruiter.net/projsame.html
Project S.A.V.E.	www.cluffassociates.com/projectsave.htm
RecruitUSA	www.recruitusa.com
Recruiters Alliance	www.recruitersalliance.com
Recruiters Café	www.recruiterscafe.com
Recruiters for Christ	www.edmondspersonnel.com
Recruiters Network	www.recruitersnetwork.com
Recruiters Online Network	www.recruitersonline.com
RecruitSoft (iLogos)	www.recruitsoft.com
The Regional Technical Recruiter's Association	www.rtra.com
ResumeBlaster	www.resumeblaster.com
ResumeXPRESS	www.resumexpress.com
Resume-Link	http://resume-link.com
Resume Monkey	www.resumemonkey.com
Resume Network	www.resume-network.com
ResumeRabbit.com	www.resumerabbit.com
Resumes on the Web	www.resweb.com
Resume Workz	www.resumeworkz.com
Resumix Internet Recruiter	www.irecruiter.com
Sacremento Area Human Resources Association	www.sahra.org
San Francisco Bay Area ASA	www.sfasa.org/joblist.html
Semco	www.semcoenterprises.com
SHRM Atlanta	www.shrmatlanta.org
SHRM Jacksonville	www.shrmjax.org
The Smart POST Network	www.smartpost.com
✣ Society for Human Resource Management HRJobs	www.shrm.org/jobs
Southeast Employment Network	www.senetwork.com
SplitIt.com	www.splitit.com
SplitJobs.com	www.splitjobs.com
Technical Recruiters Network	www.trnchicago.org
Terra Starr Technical Recruiting Network	www.terrastarr.com/trn/index.html
Texas Association of Staffing	www.texasstaffing.org
Tiburon Group	www.tiburongroup.com
Top Echelon Recruiters	www.topechelon.com
UpSeek	www.upseek.com
VacancyFinder.co.uk [United Kingdom]	www.vacancyfinder.co.uk
Virtual Relocation	www.virtualrelocation.com
Washington Area Recruiters Network	www.warn.net
WebHire Network	www.webhire.com
WEDDLE's Newsletters, Guides & Directories	**www.weddles.com**

Notes
Favorite sites, useful resources

Recruiters Resources (continued)

Wisconsin Technical Recruiters Network	www.witrn.org
You Achieve	www.youachieve.com
ZillionResumes.com	www.zillionresumes.com

Recruitment Advertising-Non-Newspaper Print & Online

Adsearch	www.adsearch.com
Advertising Age's Online Job Bank	http://adage.com/job_bank/index.html
American Journalism Review Online	www.newslink.org/joblink.html
American Medical Association Journal of the AMA (JAMA) Physician Recruitment Ads	www.ama-assn.org/sci-pubs/md_recr/md_recr.htm
American Psychological Association Monitor Classified Advertising	www.apa.org/ads
Association for Computing Machinery Career Resource Center	http://career.acm.org/crc
Bernard Hodes Group	www.hodes.com
Cell Press Online	www.cellpress.com
Chronicle of Higher Education Academe This Week	http://chronicle.merit.edu/jobs
Chronicle of Philanthropy	http://philanthropy.com/
CMPnet	www.cmpnet.com
Contract Employment Weekly Jobs Online	www.ceweekly.com
Engineering News Record	www.enr.com
The ePages Classifieds	www.ep.com
Heart Advertising	www.career.com
InformationWeek Career	www.informationweek.com/career
ITWorld.com's IT Careers	www.itcareers.com
E&P Classifieds	http://epclassifieds.com/EPM/home.html
Louisville Internet Business Directory	www.beyondbis.com/lsvdir.html
Main Street On-Line Classifieds Service	http://classifieds.maine.com
Oil Online	www.oilonline.com
Online Help Wanted	www.ohw.com
Prospect City	www.prospectcity.com
RegionalHelpWanted.com	www.regionalhelpwanted.com
Shaker Advertising	www.shaker.com
SocietyGuardian.co.uk [United Kingdom]	www.society.guardian.co.uk
Star Recruiting	www.starrecruiting.net
THESIS: The Times Higher Education Supplement InterView Service [United Kingdom]	www.thesis.co.uk
TMP Worldwide	www.tmp.com
Yahoo's Classifieds	http://classifieds.yahoo.com

Notes
Favorite sites, useful resources

Regional-USA
Alabama
Alabama Jobs	www.alabamajobs.com
Alabama Live	www.alabamalive.com
Alabama's Job Bank	www.dir.state.al.us/es
AuburnOpelikaHelpWanted.com	www.auburnopelikahelpwanted.com
Biotechnology Association of Alabama	www.bioalabama.com
BirminghamHelpWanted.com	www.birminghamhelpwanted.com
Birmingham News	www.bhnews.com
DothanHelpWanted.com	www.dothanhelpwanted.com
HuntsvilleHelpWanted.com	www.huntsvillehelpwanted.com
Huntsville Times	www.htimes.com
Links to Television Sites	http://webcom.net/~klg/alabama_tv_jobs.html
MobileHelpWanted.com	www.mobilehelpwanted.com
Mobile Register Online	www.mobileregister.com
Montgomery Advertiser	www.montgomeryadvertiser.com
MontgomeryAreaHelpWanted.com	www.montgomeryareahelpwanted.com
The Tuscaloosa News	www.tuscaloosanews.com

Alaska
ADN	www.adn.com
Alaska Fishing Jobs	www.fishingjobs.com
Alaska's Job Bank	www.labor.state.ak.us/esjobs/Jobs
Anchorage Daily News	www.adn.com/classads/ads/today/employment_index.html
AnchorageHelpWanted.com	www.anchoragehelpwanted.com
Fairbanks Daily News	http://fairbanks.abracat.com
FairbanksHelpWanted.com	www.fairbankshelpwanted.com
Frontiersman	www.frontiersman.com/class
I Love Alaska	www.ilovealaska.com/alaskajobs
Juneau Empire	www.juneauempire.com
Nome Nugget	www.nomenugget.com

Arizona
Arizona Daily Sun (Flagstaff)	www.azdailysun.com
ArizonaFamily.com	www.arizonafamily.com
Arizona Hospital and Healthcare Association AZHealthJobs	www.azhha.org
Arizona Jobs	www.arizonajobs.com
AZ-Jobs	www.az-jobs.com

Notes
Favorite sites, useful resources

Regional-USA (continued)

Arizona (continued)
The Daily Courier (Prescott)	www.prescottaz.com
East Valley Tribune (Mesa)	www.arizonatribune.com
HelpWantedPhoenix.com	www.helpwantedphoenix.com
Jobing.com	www.jobing.com
LocalCareers.com	www.localcareers.com
Pheonix Employment	www.phoenixemployment.com
Phoenix Jobs	www.phoenixjobs.com
Phoenix News Times	www.phoenixnewstimes.com
Phoenix One Stop Career Center	www.ci.phoenix.az.us
Today's News-Herald (Lake Havasu City)	www.havasunews.com
TucsonHelpWanted.com	www.tucsonhelpwanted.com
Work in Arizona	www.workinarizona.com

Arkansas
Arkansas Democrat (Little Rock)	www.ardemgaz.com
Arkansas Human Resources Association	www.ahra.org
Arkansas Jobs	www.arkansasjobs.com
Arkansas Jobs	www.arjobs.com
Benton Courier	www.bentoncourier.com
HotSpringsHelpWanted.com	www.hotspringshelpwanted.com
Jonesboro Sun	www.jonesborosun.com
LittleRockHelpWanted.com	www.littlerockhelpwanted.com
Ozark Spectator	www.ozarkspectator.com
RiverValleyHelpWanted.com	www.rivervalleyhelpwanted.com
The Sentinel-Record (Hot Springs)	www.hotsr.com
TexarkanaHelpWanted.com	www.texarkanahelpwanted.com
University of Arkansas	www.uark.edu
What A Job	www.whatajob.com

California
680 Careers.com	www.680careers.com
Abag	www.abag.ca.gov
BAJobs	www.bajobs.com
BakersfieldHelpWanted.com	www.bakersfieldhelpwanted.com
Bay Area Bioscience Center	www.bayareabioscience.org
Bay Area Careers	www.bayareacareers.com
BayAreaHelpWanted.com	www.bayareahelpwanted.com
California Agricultural Technical Institute ATI-Net AgJobs	www.atinet.org/jobs.asp
California Career & Employment Center	http://webcom.com/-career
CaliforniaCoastHelpWanted.com	www.californiacoasthelpwanted.com
California Dental Hygienists' Association Employment Opportunities	www.cdha.org/advertising/adpage.html

Notes
Favorite sites, useful resources

Regional-USA (continued)
California (continued)

California Job Network	www.cajobs.com
CaliforniaJobs.com	www.californiajobs.com
California Journalism Online	www.csne.org
California Mortgage Brokers Association Career Center	www.cambweb.org
California Separation Science Society	www.casss,org
California State University - Chico	www.csuchico.edu/plc/jobs.html
CentralCoastHelpWanted.com	www.centralcoasthelpwanted.com
ChicoHelpWanted.com	www.chicohelpwanted.com
City Java	www.cityjava.org
Coastline	www.ventura.com
☒ Craigslist	www.craigslist.com
DesertHelpWanted.com	www.deserthelpwanted.com
Fat Job	www.fatjob.com
FinancialJobs.com	www.financialjobs.com
Foothill-De Anza Community College	www.foothill.fhda.edu
Forty Plus	http://web.sirius.com/~40plus/#contact
Go Job Zone	www.gojobzone.com
HighDesertHelpWanted.com	www.highdeserthelpwanted.com
Human Resource Independent Consultants (HRIC) On-Line Job Leads	www.hric.org/hric/hrcaopp1.html
JobConnect.org	www.jobconnect.org
Job Meister	www.jobmeister.com
LA Working World	www.workingworld.com
LocalCareers.com	www.localcareers.com
LosAngelesHelpWanted.com	www.losangeleshelpwanted.com
Los Angeles Times	www.latimes.com
MercedHelpWanted.com	www.mercedhelpwanted.com
Mercury Center	www.sjmercury.com
Mercury News (San Jose)	www.bayarea.com
ModestoHelpWanted.com	www.modestohelpwanted.com
MontereyBayHelpWanted.com	www.montereybayhelpwanted.com
NACCB Southern California Chapter	www.socal-naccb.org
Netcom	www.netcom.com
NorthBayCareers.com	www.northbaycareers.com
NorthBayHelpWanted.com	www.northbayhelpwanted.com
Orange County Register	www.ocregister.com
Palo Alto Weekly	www.service.com/PAW/home.html
Professionals in Human Resource Association Career Center	www.pihra.org/capirasn/careers.nsf/home?open

Notes
Favorite sites, useful resources

Regional-USA (continued)
California (continued)
Presidio Jobs	www.presidio-jobs.com
ReddingHelpWanted.com	www.reddinghelpwanted.com
Sacramento Bee	www.sacbee.com
SacramentoHelpWanted.com	www.sacramentohelpwanted.com
Sacramento Human Resource Management Association	www.shrma.org
Sacramento Recruiter	www.sacramentorecruiter.com
San Diego Careers	www.sandiegocareers.com
San Diego Jobs	www.sandiegojobs.com
San Diego Software Industry Council	www.sdsic.org
San Francisco Chronicle	www.sfgate.com
San Francisco Bay Area American Staffing Association	www.sfasa.org/joblist.html
San Francisco Bay Area Job Hub	www.jobhub.com
San Francisco State University Instructional Technologies	www.itec.sfsu.edu
Sonic Net	www.sonic.net/employment
SonomaCountyHelpWanted.com	www.sonomacountyhelpwanted.com
Southern California	www.so-cal-jobs.com
Southern California Electronic Data Interchange Roundtable	www.scedir.org/html/jobs.html
StocktonHelpWanted.com	www.stocktonhelpwanted.com
University of California- Berkeley Work-Study Programs	http://workstudy.berkeley.edu
The Valley Exchange	www.thevalleyexchange.com

Colorado
Aspen Daily News	www.aspendailynews.com
CareersColorado.com	www.careerscolorado.com
Colorado Computerwork	http://colorado.computerwork.com
Colorado Health and Hospital Association	www.cha.com
Colorado Human Resource Association Online	www.chra.org
Colorado Online Job Connection	www.peakweb.com
ColoradoSpringsHelpWanted.com	www.coloradospringshelpwanted.com
Colorado Springs Independent	www.csindy.com
Colorado Springs Society for Human Resource Management	www.csshrm.org
Colorado Technical Recruiters Network	www.ctrn.org/ctrn.org
The Daily Sentinel (Grand Junction)	www.gjsentinel.com
Denver Post	www.denverpost.com
Durango Herald	www.durangoherald.com

Notes
Favorite sites, useful resources

Regional-USA (continued)
Colorado (continued)
HighCountryHelpWanted.com	www.highcountryhelpwanted.com
Inside Denver	www.insidedenver.com/jobs
NorthernColoradoHelpWanted.com	www.northerncoloradohelpwanted.com
RockyMountainHelpWanted.com	www.rockymountainhelpwanted.com
State of Colorado	www.state.co.us
WesternSlopeHelpWanted.com	www.westernslopehelpwanted.com

Connecticut
The Advocate (Stamford)	www.stamfordadvocate.com
Connecticut's BioScience Cluster	www.curenet.org
CT High Tech	www.cthightech.com
CT Jobs	www.ctjobs.com
Danbury News-Times	www.newstimes.com
Fairfield, CT Jewish Jobs	www.jewishjobs.com
FairfieldCountyHelpWanted.com	www.fairfieldcountyhelpwanted.com
FairfieldCountyJobs.com	www.fairfieldcountyjobs.com
Hartford Courant	www.ctnow.com
HartfordHelpWanted.com	www.hartfordhelpwanted.com
New England Job	www.jobct.com
NewHavenHelpWanted.com	www.newhavenhelpwanted.com
New Haven Register	www.newhavenregister.com
Tri-StateJobs.com	www.tristatejobs.com
Waterbury Republican American	wws.rep-am.com

Delaware
Delaware's Employment	www.delmarweb.com
Delaware Online	http://jobs.delawareonline.com/index.shtml
Delaware Valley Technical Recruiters Network	www.dvtrn.org
DelmarvaHelpWanted.com	www.delmarvahelpwanted.com
Dover Post	www.doverpost.com
JobCircle	www.jobcircle.com
JobNet	www.jobnet.com
The News Journal (Wilmington)	www.delawareonline.com
Opportunity Center, Inc.	www.oppctr.com
Tri-State	www.tri-state-hr.org
Virtual Career Network	www.vcnet.net

Help Someone in Transition. ☛ WEDDLE's 2004 Job Seeker's Guide.

Notes
Favorite sites, useful resources

Regional-USA (continued)

District of Columbia
The Catholic University of America Career Services Office	http://careers.cua.edu/studalum/progserv.htm
dcaccountingjobs.com	www.dcaccountingjobs.com
DC Job Source	http://dcjobsource.com
DC Registry	www.dcregistry.com
HelpWantedDC.com	www.helpwanteddc.com
Human Resource Association of the National Capital Area Job Bank Listing	http://hra-nca.org/job_list.asp
WashingtonJobs.com	www.washingtonjobs.com
The Washington Post	www.washingtonpost.com
Washington Times	www.washtimes.com

East Coast
East Bay Works	www.eastbayworks.org
East Coast Jobs	www.eastcoastjobs.net
Planet Tech	www.planet-tech.net

Florida
1-Jobs.com	www.1-jobs.com
BioFlorida	www.bioflorida.com
Central Florida Human Resource Association	www.cfhra.org
CoastalHelpWanted.com	www.coastalhelpwanted.com
DaytonaHelpWanted.com	www.daytonahelpwanted.com
EmeraldCoastHelpWanted.com	www.emeraldcoasthelpwanted.com
Florida CareerLINK	www.floridacareerlink.com
Florida Jobs	www.floridajobs.com
Florida Jobs Online!	www.florida-jobs-online.com
Florida-Jobs.net	www.florida-jobs.net
Florida NACCB	www.floridanaccb.org
Florida Times Union (Jacksonville)	www.jacksonville.com
GainesvilleOcalaHelpWanted.com	www.gainesvilleocalahelpwanted.com
HeartlandHelpWanted.com	www.heartlandhelpwanted.com
Human Resource Association of Broward County	www.hrabc.org
JacksonvilleHelpWanted.com	www.jacksonvillehelpwanted.com
Miami Herald	www.miami.com
Miami Jobs	www.miami-jobs.net
Mondo Jobs	www.mondojobs.com
Nova Southeastern University	www.nova.edu
OrlandoHelpWanted.com	www.orlandohelpwanted.com
Orlando Jobs	www.orlando-jobs.com
Orlando Sentinel	www.orlandosentinel.com

Notes
Favorite sites, useful resources

Regional-USA (continued)
Florida (continued)
PanamaCityHelpWanted.com	www.panamacityhelpwanted.com
PensacolaHelpWanted.com	www.pensacolahelpwanted.com
Pensacola News Journal	www.pensacolanewstimes.com
RhinoMite	www.rhinomite.com
St. Petersburg Times	www.sptimes.com
SHRM Jacksonville	www.shrmjax.org
SoFla.com	www.sofla.com
SouthwestFloridaHelpWanted.com	www.southwestfloridahelpwanted.com
SpaceCoastHelpWanted.com	www.spacecoasthelpwanted.com
Sun-Sentinel Career Path	www.sun-sentinel.com/Careerpath
TallahasseeHelpWanted.com	www.tallahasseehelpwanted.com
Tampa Bay Employment	www.tampabaywired.com
Tampa Jobs.com	www.tampa-jobs.com
WestPalmBeachHelpWanted.com	www.westpalmbeachhelpwanted.com

Georgia
The Albany Herald	www.albanyh.surfsouth.com
Atlanta Human Resources Association	www.harb.net/ahra
Atlanta Job Resource Center	www.ajrc.com
Atlanta-Jobs	www.atlanta-jobs.com
Atlanta Journal and Constitution	www.accessatlanta.com
Augusta Chronicle	www.augustachronicle.com
AugustaHelpWanted.com	www.augustahelpwanted.com
ChattahoocheeHelpWanted.com	www.chattahoocheehelpwanted.com
Emory University Rollins School of Public Health	www.sph.emory.edu/studentservice
Georgia Association of Personnel Services	www.jobconnection.com/specialty
Georgia Careers	www.georgiajobs.net
Georgia Pharmacy Association	www.gpha.org
Georgia State University Career Services	www.gsu.edu/dept/admin/plc/homepage4.html
Georgia Tech Career Services Office	www.career.gatech.edu
Job Net	www.westga.edu/~coop
Macon Telegraph	www.macon.com

Notes
Favorite sites, useful resources

Regional-USA (continued)
Georgia (continued)
MidGeorgiaHelpWanted.com	www.midgeorgiahelpwanted.com
National Association of Securities Professionals (Atlanta) Current Openings	www.naspatlanta.com/career.html
NW Georgia Careers	www.careerdepot.org
SavannahHelpWanted.com	www.savannahhelpwanted.com
Savannah Morning News	www.savannahnow.com
SHRM Atlanta	www.shrmatlanta.org
SoutheastGeorgiaHelpWanted.com	www.southeastgeorgiahelpwanted.com
SouthwestGeorgiaHelpWanted.com	www.southwestgeorgiahelpwanted.com
The Southeastern Employment Network	www.senetwork.com
SouthwestGeorgiaHelpWanted.com	www.southwestgeorgiahelpwanted.com

Hawaii
Hawaii Techies	www.hawaii.techies.com
Hawaii Tribune-Herald (Hilo)	www.hilohawaiitribune.com
Honolulu Advertiser	www.honoluluadvertiser.com
HonoluluHelpWanted.com	www.honoluluhelpwanted.com
Honolulu Star-Bulletin	www.starbulletin.com
Jobs Hawaii	www.jobshawaii.com
Maui.net	www.maui.net
Maui News	www.mauinews.com
Starbulletin	www.starbulletin.com
West Hawaii Today (Kailua)	www.westhawaiitoday.com

Idaho
BoiseHelpWanted.com	www.boisehelpwanted.com
Cedar Rapids Gazette	www.gazetteonline.com
The Daily Nonpareil (Council Bluffs)	www.nonpareilonline.com
Des Moines Register	www.dmregister.com
Idaho Careers	www.idahocareers.com
Idaho Department of Labor	www.labor.state.id.us/
Quad City Times (Davenport)	www.qctimes.com
Sioux City Journal	www.trib.com/scjournal

Illinois
Accountant Jobs Chicago	www.accountantjobschicago.com
Audit Jobs Chicago	www.auditjobschicago.com
CapitalHelpWanted.com	www.capitalhelpwanted.com

Notes
Favorite sites, useful resources

Regional-USA (continued)

Illinois (continued)

CentralIllinoisHelpWanted.com	www.centralillinoishelpwanted.com
Chicago AMA	http://chicagoama.org
Chicago Jobs	www.chicagojobs.org
Chicago Software Newspaper	www.chisoft.com
Chicago Tribune	www.chicagotribune.com
Chicagoland's Virtual Job Resource	www.staffsolutions.com
Engineering Job Source	www.engineerjobs.com
FetchMeAJob.com	www.fetchmeajob.com
Herald & Review (Decatur)	www.herald-review.com
Human Resource Association of Greater Oak Brook	http://members.aol.com/hraob/main.htm
ILJobs.com	www.iljobs.com
IlliniHelpWanted.com	www.illinihelpwanted.com
Illinois CPA Society Career Center	www.icpas.org/icpas/career-services/carsrce.asp
IllinoisJobs.com	www.illinoisjobs.com
Job Force Network	www.jobforce.net
Jobs in Chicago	www.jobsinchicago.com
Loyola College	www.lattanze.loyola.edu
The News-Gazette (Champaigne)	www.news-gazette.com
PeoriaHelpWanted.com	www.peoriahelpwanted.com
The Regional Technical Recruiter's Association	www.rtra.com
Register-News (Mount Vernon)	www.register-news.com
Sorkins Job Bank	www.sorkinsjobbank.com
The State Journal Register (Springfield)	www.sj-r.com
SuburbanChicagoHelpWanted.com	www.suburbanchicagohelpwanted.com
Tax Jobs Chicago	www.taxjobschicago.com
Terra Starr Technical Recruiting Network	www.terra-starr.com/trn/index.html
University of Chicago	www.uchicago.edu/alum/index.html

Indiana

CentralIndianaHelpWanted.com	www.centralindianahelpwanted.com
Engineering Job Source	www.engineerjobs.com
The Evansville Courier	http://ads.evansville.net/employment
FetchMeAJob.com	www.fetchmeajob.com
Indiana Engineering and Technical Opportunities	www.engineerjobs.com/in_jobs.html
The Herald-Times (Bloomington)	www.hoosiertimes.com

Notes
Favorite sites, useful resources

Regional-USA (continued)
Indiana (continued)

Indiana Jobs	www.indianajobs.com
Indiana Jobs	http://rking.vinu.edu/injobs.htm
IndianapolisHelpWanted.com	www.indianapolishelpwanted.com
Indianapolis Star News	www.indystar.com
Indy Mall	www.indymall.com/class-ad/employmt.htm
The News-Sentinel (Fort Wayne)	www.fortwayne.com
Online Jobs Indiana	www.circlecity.com/jobs/index.html
Purdue University Management Placement Office	www.mgmt.purdue.edu/departments/gcs/
Post-Tribune (Gary)	www.post-trib.com
SouthBendHelpWanted.com	www.southbendhelpwanted.com
South Bend Tribune	www.sbinfo.com
TerreHauteHelpWanted.com	www.terrehautehelpwanted.com
TriStateHelpWanted.com	www.tristatehelpwanted.com

Iowa

CedarRapidsIowaCityHelpWanted.com	www.cedarrapidsiowacityhelpwanted.com
CentralIowaHelpWanted.com	www.centraliowahelpwanted.com
Corridor Careers	www.corridorcareers.com
DesMoinesHelpWanted.com	www.desmoineshelpwanted.com
DesMoines Register	www.dmregister.com/jobcity/index.html
Drake University	www.drake.edu
DubuqueHelpWanted.com	www.dubuquehelpwanted.com
Dubuque Iowa	www.dubuque-ia.com/jobs.cfm
FortDodgeHelpWanted.com	www.fortdodgehelpwanted.com
Iowa Biotechnology Association	www.iowabiotech.org
Iowa Jobs	www.state.ia.us/jobs/index.html
NorthernIowaHelpWanted.com	www.northerniowahelpwanted.com
Our Dubuque	www.dubuque-ia.com/jobs.cfm
SiouxLandHelpWanted.com	www.siouxlandhelpwanted.com
SouthernIowaHelpWanted.com	www.southerniowahelpwanted.com

Notes
Favorite sites, useful resources

Regional-USA (continued)

Kansas
access Kansas	www.accesskansas.org
Daily Union (Junction City)	www.dailyu.com
Kansas City Kansan	www.kansascitykansan.com
Kansas Jobs	www.kansasjobs.org
Salina Journal	www.saljournal.com
Sorkins Job Bank	www.sorkinsjobbank.com
The Topeka Capital Journal	www.cjonline.com
TopekaHelpWanted.com	www.topekahelpwanted.com
Wichita Eagle	www.kansas.com
WichitaHelpWanted.com	www.wichitahelpwanted.com

Kentucky
The Courier-Journal (Louisville)	www.courier-journal.com
The Daily News (Bowling Green)	www.bgdailynews.com
Grayson County News-Gazette (Leitchfield)	www.gcnewsgazette.com
HelpWantedLexington.com	www.helpwantedlexington.com
HuntingtonAshlandHelpWanted.com	www.huntingtonashlandhelpwanted.com
KentuckyJobs.com	www.kentuckyjobs.com
Lexington Herald Leader	www.kentucky.com
LouisvilleHelpWanted.com	www.louisvillehelpwanted.com
Louisville Internet Business Directory	www.beyondbis.com/lsvdir.html
Sentinel News (Shelbyville)	www.shelbyconnect.com

Louisiana
AcadianaHelpWanted.com	www.acadianahelpwanted.com
The Advocate (Baton Rouge)	www.advocate.com
BatonRougeHelpWanted.com	www.batonrougehelpwanted.com
CenLAHelpWanted.com	www.cenlahelpwanted.com
Info Louisiana	www.state.la.us
The Jackson Independent (Jonesboro)	www.jackson-ind.com
Med Job Louisiana	www.medjoblouisiana.com/code.htm
MonroeHelpWanted.com	www.monroehelpwanted.com
Natchitouches Times	www.natchitouchestimes.com
NewOrleansHelpWanted.com	www.neworleanshelpwanted.com
Northwest Louisiana Society for Human Resource Management	www.softdisk.com/customer/nwlashrm
ShreveportHelpWanted.com	www.shreveporthelpwanted.com
The Times (Shreveport)	www.shreveporttimes.com
The Times-Picayune (New Orleans)	www.nola.com

Notes
Favorite sites, useful resources

WEDDLE's Helping to Maximize Your ROI ... Your Return on the Internet

Regional-USA (continued)
Maine
Bangor Daily News	www.bangornews.com
Biotechnology Association of Maine	www.mainebiotech.org
CentralMaineHelpWanted.com	www.centralmainehelpwanted.com
EasternMaineHelpWanted.com	www.easternmainehelpwanted.com
◕ Jobs in Maine	www.jobsinme.com
Kennebec Journal (Augusta)	www.kjonline.com
Lewiston Sun Journal	www.sunjournal.com
Maine Employment Board	www.spruceharbor.com/welcome/mejobs.htm
Maine-Job.com	www.maine-job.com
Maine Street On-Line Classifieds Service	http://classifieds.maine.com
Portland Press Herald	www.portland.com
SouthernMaineHelpWanted.com	www.southernmainehelpwanted.com
The Times Record (Brunswick)	www.timesrecord.com

Maryland
BaltimoreHelpWanted.com	www.baltimorehelpwanted.com
Baltimore Sun	www.sunspot.net
The Capital (Annapolis)	www.hometownannapolis.com
Chesapeake Human Resource Association	www.chra.com
FrederickHelpWanted.com	www.frederickhelpwanted.com
The Herald-Mail (Hagerstown)	www.herald-mail.com
Human Resource Association of the National Capital Area Job Bank Listing	http://hra-nca.org/job_list.asp
Maryland Association of CPAs Job Connect	www.macpa.org/services/jobconnt/index.htm
Maryland Jobs	www.Maryland-jobs.com
Maryland Times-Press (Ocean City)	www.marylandtimespress.com
MdBio, Inc. (Maryland Bioscience)	www.mdbio.org
Sailor	http://sailor.lib.md.us
The Star Democrat (Easton)	www.stardem.com
WashingtonJobs.com	www.washingtonjobs.com

Massachusetts
Boston Online Employment	www.boston-online.com/Employment/
The Boston Globe	www.boston.com
Boston Hire	www.bostonhire.com
Boston Job Bank	www.bostonjobs.com
BostonSearch.com	www.bostonsearch.com

www.WEDDLES.com   253

Notes
Favorite sites, useful resources

Regional-USA (continued)

Massachusetts (continued)

CapeAndIslandsHelpWanted.com	www.capeandislandshelpwanted.com
The Eagle-Tribune (Lawrence)	www.eagletribune.com
HelpWantedBoston.com	www.helpwantedboston.com
JVS Career Moves	www.jvsjobs.org
Massachusetts Biotechnology Council	www.massbio.org
Massachusetts' Jobs	www.Massachusetts-jobs.com
Personnel Management Association of Western New England	www.pmawne.org
SpringfieldHelpWanted.com	www.springfieldhelpwanted.com
The Sun (Lowell)	www.lowellsun.com
The Salem News	www.salemnews.com
Town Online	http://townonline.com
Union-News & Sunday Republican (Springfield)	www.masslive.com
Worchester Polytechnic Institute	www.wpi.edu

Michigan

Ann Arbor News	www.annarbornews.com
Detroit Free Press	www.freep.com
Engineering Job Source	www.engineerjobs.com
FetchMeAJob.com	www.fetchmeajob.com
FlintHelpWanted.com	www.flinthelpwanted.com
Flint Journal	www.flintjournal.com
GrandRapidsHelpWanted.com	www.grandrapidshelpwanted.com
Grand Rapids Press	www.gr-press.com
Human Resource Management Association of Mid Michigan Job Postings	http://hrmamm.com/jobs.asp
Lansing State Journal	www.lansingstatejournal.com
MichBIO	www.michbio.org
Michigan CareerSite	http://jobs.michigan.org
Michigan Job Hunter	www.michiganjobhunter.com
MichiganJobs.com	www.michiganjobs.com
Michigan-Online	www.michigan-online.com
Michigan Pharmacists Association	www.mipharm.com
Michigan Talent Bank	www.michworks.org
Michigan Web	http://michiganweb.com/empagency.html
MidMichiganHelpWanted.com	www.midmichiganhelpwanted.com
MotorCityHelpWanted.com	www.motorcityhelpwanted.com
MuskegonHelpWanted.com	www.muskegonhelpwanted.com
Oakland University	www2.oakland.edu/careerservices

Notes
Favorite sites, useful resources

Regional-USA (continued)
Michigan (continued)
Pride Source	www.pridesource.com
SouthwestMichiganJobs.com	www.southwestmichiganjobs.com
UpperPeninsulaHelpWanted.com	www.upperpeninsulahelpwanted.com

Midwest
JobsintheMidwest.com	www.jobsinthemidwest.com
MidWest Career Matrix	www.careermatrix.com

Minnesota
Duluth News-Tribune	www.duluthsuperior.com
Elk River Star News	www.erstarnews.com
The Journal (New Ulm)	www.oweb.com/NewUlm/journal/home.html
HelpWantedRochester.com	www.helpwantedrochester.com
Hennepin County Job Openings	www.co.hennepin.mn.us/jobs/jobs.htm
MinJobs.com	www.minjobs.com
Minneapolis Jobs	www.minneapolis-jobs.com
Minneapolis Star Tribune	www.startribune.com
Minnesota Jobs	www.mn-jobs.com
MinnesotaJobs.com	www.minnesotajobs.com
Minnesota Technical Recruiters Network	www.psijobfair.com/trn
NorthlandHelpWanted.com	www.northlandhelpwanted.com
SouthernMinnesotaHelpWanted.com	www.southernminnesotahelpwanted.com
StCloudHelpWanted.com	www.stcloudhelpwanted.com
Saint Paul Pioneer Press	www.twincities.com
TwinCitiesHelpWanted.com	www.twincitieshelpwanted.com

Mississippi
CentralMississippiHelpWanted.com	www.centralmississippihelpwanted.com
The Clarion Ledger (Jackson)	www.clarionledger.com
GulfCoastHelpWanted.com	www.gulfcoasthelpwanted.com
MeridianHelpWanted.com	www.meridianhelpwanted.com
Meridian Star	www.meridianstar.com
Mississippi Careers	www.misscareers.com
The Natchez Democrat	www.natchezdemocrat.com
The Sun Herald (Biloxi)	www.sunherald.com
TupeloHelpWanted.com	www.tupelohelpwanted.com
The Vicksburg Post	www.vicksburgpost.com

WEDDLE's Helping to Maximize Your ROI ... Your Return on the Internet

Notes
Favorite sites, useful resources

WEDDLE's Helping to Maximize Your ROI ... Your Return on the Internet

Regional-USA (continued)
Missouri
The Examiner (Independence)	www.examiner.net
Hannibal Courier-Post	www.hannibal.net
HeartlandJobs.com	www.heartlandjobs.com
Human Resource Management Association of Greater Kansas City	http://hrma-kc.org
Jefferson City News Tribune	www.newstribune.com
Joplin Globe	www.joplinglobe.com
Kansas City.com	www.kansascity.com
KansasCityHelpWanted.com	www.kansascityhelpwanted.com
Kansas City Jobs	www.kansascity-jobs.com
Missouri Association of Personnel Services	www.moaps.com
Missouri Pharmacy Association	www.morx.com
Missouri Works	www.works.state.mo.us
Online Columbia	www.onlinecolumbia.com/Jobsearch.asp
OzarksHelpWanted.com	www.ozarkshelpwanted.com
Springfield News-Leader	www.springfieldnews-leader.com
St. Louis Jobs	www.stlouis-jobs.co
St. Louis Virtual Job Fair	www.stltechjobs.com
Sorkins Job Bank	www.sorkinsjobbank.com

Montana
Billings Gazette	www.billingsgazette.com
BillingsHelpWanted.com	www.billingshelpwanted.com
Bozeman Daily Chronicle	www.gomontana.com
Helena Independent Record	www.helenair.com
Missoulian	www.missoulian.com
Montana Job Service	http://jsd.dli.state.mt.us
The Montana Standard (Butte)	www.mtstandard.com
SouthwestMontanaHelpWanted.com	www.southwestmontanahelpwanted.com

Nebraska
Access Omaha	www.accessomaha.com/jobs/jobs.html
Columbus Telegram	www.columbustelegram.com
CornhuskerHelpWanted.com	www.cornhuskerhelpwanted.com
Lincoln Journal Star	www.journalstar.com
North Platte Telegraph	www.nptelegraph.com
OmahaHelpWanted.com	www.omahahelpwanted.com
Omaha World-Herald	www.omaha.com
Scotts Bluff Star-Herald	www.starherald.com

Notes
Favorite sites, useful resources

Regional-USA (continued)

Nevada
Elko Daily Free Press	www.elkodaily.com
LasVegasHelpWanted.com	www.lasvegashelpwanted.com
Las Vegas Review-Journal	www.lvrj.com
Las Vegas Sun	www.lasvegassun.com
Nevada Appeal (Carson City)	www.nevadaappeal.com
Nevada Mining	www.nevadamining.org
RenoHelpWanted.com	www.renohelpwanted.com
Reno Gazette Journal	www.rgj.com

New England
Independent Human Resource Consultants Association	www.ihrca.com/Contract_Regular.asp
Jobfind.com	www.jobfind.com
New England Job	www.newenglandjob.com
New England Careers	www.newenglandcareers.com
Northeast Human Resource Association	www.nehra.org
Opportunity NOCS	www.opnocs.org
SouthernNewEnglandHelpWanted.com	www.southernnewenglandhelpwanted.com
The Search Begins Online	www.todays-careers.com

New Hampshire
Across New Hampshire	www.across-nh.com
Concord Monitor	www.concordmonitor.com
JobsinNH.com	www.jobsinnh.com
Keene Sentinel	www.keenesentinel.com
NewHampshireHelpWanted.com	www.newhampshirehelpwanted.com
New Hampshire Legal Assistance	www.nhla.org
NH.com	www.nh.com
nhjobs.com	www.nhjobs.com
Portsmouth Herald	www.seacoastonline.com
The Telegraph (Nashua)	www.nashuatelegraph.com
The Union Leader (Manchester)	www.theunionleader.com

New Jersey
Atlantic City Jobs	www.acjobs.com
Asbury Park Press	www.app.com
Biotechnology Council of New Jersey	www.newjerseybiotech.org
CareerLocal.net	www.careerlocal.net
Courier-Post (Cherry Hill)	www.courierpostonline.com
Employment Channel	www.employ.com
In Jersey	www.injersey.com
Job Circle	www.jobcircle.com

Notes
Favorite sites, useful resources

Regional-USA (continued)

New Jersey (continued)
JobNet	www.jobnet.com
The Montclair Times	www.montclairtimes.com
NewJerseyHelpWanted.com	www.newjerseyhelpwanted.com
New Jersey Human Resource Planning Group	www.njhrpg.org
New Jersey Net Connections	www.netconnections.net/nj/nj.html
New Jersey Online	www.nj.com
New Jersey Staffing Association	www.njsa.com
New Jersey Technical Recruiters Alliance	www.njtra.org
New Jersey Technology Council	www.njtc.org
New Media Association of New Jersey	www.nmanj.com
NJ Careers	www.njcareers.com
NJ Jobs	www.njjobs.com
NJPAHelpWanted.com	www.njpahelpwanted.com
NorthJerseyHelpWanted.com	www.northjerseyhelpwanted.com
Princeton Info	www.princetoninfo.com
The Star Ledger (Newark)	www.nj.com
The Trentonian	www.trentonian.com
Tri-StateJobs.com	www.tristatejobs.com

New Mexico
Albuquerque Journal	www.abqjournal.com
The Gallup Independent	www.gallupindependent.com
HelpWantedNewMexico.com	www.helpwantednewmexico.com
Los Alamos Monitor	www.lamonitor.com
New Mexico High Tech Job Forum	www.nmtechjobs.com
Santa Fe New Mexican	www.sfnewmexican.com
The Silver City Daily Press	www.thedailypress.com

New York
411 NYC Jobs	www.411nycjobs.com
AdirondackHelpWanted.com	www.adirondackhelpwanted.com
Albany Democrat Herald	www.dhonline.com
BigAppleHelpWanted.com	www.bigapplehelpwanted.com
BinghamtonHelpWanted.com	www.binghamtonhelpwanted.com
The Bookbinders Guild of New York Job Bank	www.bbgny.com//guild/jb.html
BuffaloHelpWanted.com	www.buffalohelpwanted.com
CapitalAreaHelpWanted.com	www.capitalareahelpwanted.com

Notes
Favorite sites, useful resources

Regional-USA (continued)
New York (continued)

CentralNewYorkHelpWanted.com	www.centralnewyorkhelpwanted.com
ColumbiaGreeneHelpWanted.com	www.columbiagreenehelpwanted.com
Cornell Career Services	http://student-jobs.ses.cornell.edu
daVinci Times	www.daVinciTimes.org
Employment Weekly	www.employment-weekly.com
FingerLakesHelpWanted.com	www.fingerlakeshelpwanted.com
HelpWantedLongIsland.com	www.helpwantedlongisland.com
HudsonValleyHelpWanted.com	www.hudsonvalleyhelpwanted.com
Human Resource Association of New York	www.nyshrm.org
IthacaHelpWanted.com	www.ithacahelpwanted.com
Ithaca Times	www.ithacatimes.com
Job Circle	www.jobcircle.com
Job Force NY	www.jobforceny.com
1000IslandsHelpWanted.com	www.1000islandshelpwanted.com
LI Jobs	www.lijobs.com
LocalCareers.com	www.localcareers.com
National Association of Securities Professionals (New York) Underground Railroad	www.nasp-ny.org
The New York Biotechnology Association	www.nyba.org
New York Careers	www.nycareers.com
New York Department of Labor	www.labor.state.ny.us
New York Foundation for the Arts	www.nyfa.org/opportunities.asp?type=Job&id=94&fid=6&sid=17
New York New Media Association	www.nynma.com/jobs
New York Post	www.nypost.com
New York Society of Security Analysts Career Resources	www.nyssa.org/jobs
New York State Society of CPAs	www.nysscpa.org/classified/main.cfm
New York Technical Recruiters Association	www.nytra.com
The New York Times	www.nytimes.com
New York's Preferred Jobs	www.nycityjobs.com
NY Job Source	www.nyjobsource.com
NY Preferred Jobs	http://newyork.preferredjobs.com

Notes
Favorite sites, useful resources

Regional-USA (continued)

New York (continued)
NYC Job Bank	www.nycjobbank.com
NYPAHelpWanted.com	www.nypahelpwanted.com
OleanHelpWanted.com	www.oleanhelpwanted.com
Rensselier Polytechnic Institute Career Development Center	www.cdc.rpi.edu
RochesterHelpWanted.com	www.rochesterhelpwanted.com
Rochester, NY Careers	www.rochestercareers.com
SeawayHelpWanted.com	www.seawayhelpwanted.com
SiliconAlley.com	www.siliconalley.com
Silicon Alley Daily	www.siliconalleydaily.com
SyracuseHelpWanted.com	www.syracusehelpwanted.com
SyracuseJobs	http:syracuse.jobs-employment.net
Syracuse New Times	www.newtimes.com
Syracuse Online	www.syracuse.com
Tri-StateJobs.com	www.tristatejobs.com
TwinTiersHelpWanted.com	www.twintiershelpwanted.com
US Empleos	www.usempleos.com
Westchester Jobs	www.westchesterjobs.com
Western NY JOBS	www.wnyjobs.com

North Carolina
AshevilleHelpWanted.com	www.ashevillehelpwanted.com
Career Women	www.webcom.com/~nccareer
Carolina Career Web	www.carolinascareerweb.com
Carolina Computer Jobs	www.carolinacomputerjobs.com
CharlotteHelpWanted.com	www.charlottehelpwanted.com
Charlotte Observer	www.charlotte.com
Charlotte Online	http://thiscity.com/jobs
Duke University Job Resources	http://career.studentaffairs.duke.edu
EastCarolinaHelpWanted.com	www.eastcarolinahelpwanted.com
Employment Security Commission Home Page	www.neesc.com
Greensboro News-Record	www.nowc-record.com
Job Listing Form	www.charweb.org
News & Observer (Raleigh)	www.newsobserver.com
North Carolina Biotechnology Center	www.ncbiotech.org
North Carolina Genomics & Bioinformatics Consortium	www.ncgbc.org
North Carolina JobLink Career Center	www.joblink.state.nc.us
The North Carolina Office of State Personnel	www.osp.state.nc.us
PiedmontHelpWanted.com	www.piedmonthelpwanted.com
TriangleHelpWanted.com	www.trianglehelpwanted.com

Notes
Favorite sites, useful resources

WEDDLE's Helping to Maximize Your ROI ... Your Return on the Internet

Regional-USA (continued)

North Carolina (continued)
Welcome to North Carolina	www.ncgov.com
Wilmington Star	www.wilmingtonstar.com
Winston-Salem Journal	www.journalnow.com

North Dakota
BismarckMandanHelpWanted.com	www.bismarckmandenhelpwanted.com
Bismarck Tribune	www.bismarcktribune.com
FargoJobs.com	www.fargojobs.com
Grand Forks Herald	www.grandforks.com
The Jamestown Sun	www.jamestownsun.com
Minot Daily News	www.minotdailynews.com

Ohio
CareerBoard	www.careerboard.com
Case Western Reserve University	www.cwru.edu
Cincinnati Enquirer	www.enquirer.com
Cincinnati/Jobs	http://careerfinder.cincinnati.com
Cleveland Careers	www.cleveland.com
ClevelandHelpWanted.com	www.clevelandhelpwanted.com
The Cleveland Nation	www.clnation.com
Columbus Dispatch	www.dispatch.com
ColumbusHelpWanted.com	www.columbushelpwanted.com
Dayton Daily News	www.daytondailynews.com
DaytonHelpWanted.com	www.daytonhelpwanted.com
FetchMeAJob.com	www.fetchmeajob.com
HelpWantedCincinnati.com	www.helpwantedcincinnati.com
MahoningValleyHelpWanted.com	www.mahoningvalleyhelpwanted.com
MansfieldAreaHelpWanted.com	www.mansfieldareahelpwanted.com
Ohio Careers Resource Center	www.ohiocareers.com
Ohio Job Prospector	www.jobprospector.com
Ohio State Council	www.ohioshrm.org
SoutheasternOhioHelpWanted.com	www.southeasternohiohelpwanted.com
Springfield News Sun	www.springfieldnewssun.com
ToledoHelpWanted.com	www.toledohelpwanted.com
TriStateJobMatch.com (Monster.com)	www.tristatejobmatch.com

Oklahoma
Altus Times	www.altustimes.com
Lawton Constitution	www.lawton-constitution.com
OKC - Cityhall.org	www.okc-cityhall.org

Notes
Favorite sites, useful resources

Regional-USA (continued)

Oklahoma (continued)

OklahomaCityHelpWanted.com	www.oklahomacityhelpwanted.com
Oklahoma Jobs	www.oklahoma-jobs.com
The Oklahoman (Oklahoma City)	www.newsok.com
Ponca City News	www.poncacitynews.com
Tulsa Area Human Resources Association	www.tahra.org
TulsaHelpWanted.com	www.tulsahelpwanted.com
Tulsa World	www.tulsaworld.com

Oregon

CentralOregonJobs.com	www.centraloregonjobs.com
Columbia-Willamette Compensation Group	www.cwcg.org
East Oregonian (Pendleton)	www.eonow.com
EugeneHelpWanted.com	www.eugenehelpwanted.com
Hiregate.com	www.hiregate.com
Oregon Bioscience Association	www.oregon-bioscience.com
Oregon Education Jobs	www.edjobs.net
Oregon Employment Department	www.emp.state.or.us
The Oregonian (Portland)	www.oregonian.com
PortlandHelpWanted.com	www.portlandhelpwanted.com
Portland Jobs	www.portland-jobs.com
The Portland Human Resource Management Assn	www.pdxnhrmashrm.org
The Register-Guard (Eugene)	www.registerguard.com
SouthernOregonHelpWanted.com	www.southernoregonhelpwanted.com
Springfield News	www.hometownnews.com
Statesman Journal (Salem)	www.statesmanjournal.copm

Pennsylvania

CentreCountyHelpWanted.com	www.centrecountyhelpwanted.com
ClearfieldJeffersonHelpWanted.com	www.clearfieldjeffersonhelpwanted.com
Drexel University	www.drexel.edu/scdc/
Erie Daily Times-News	www.goerie.com
ErieHelpWanted.com	www.eriehelpwanted.com
HelpWantedTriState.com	www.helpwantedtristate.com
Job Circle	www.jobcircle.com
JobNet	www.jobnet.com
JohnstownHelpWanted.com	www.johnstownhelpwanted.com
KeystoneHelpWanted.com	www.keystonehelpwanted.com
LehighValleyHelpWanted.com	www.lehighvalleyhelpwanted.com
Pennsylvania Jobs	www.pennsylvaniajobs.com

Notes
Favorite sites, useful resources

Regional-USA (continued)

Pennsylvania (continued)
The Philadelphia Inquirer	www.philly.com
Philadelphia-Jobs	www.philadelphia-jobs.com
PhiladelphiaHelpWanted.com	www.philadelphiahelpwanted.com
PhillyWorks	www.phillyworks.com
PittsburghHelpWanted.com	www.pittsburghhelpwanted.com
PittsburghJobs	www.pittsburghjobs.com
Pittsburgh Personnel Association	www.ppapitt.org
Pittsburg Post-Gazette	www.post-gazette.com
Scranton Times Tribune	www.scrantontimes.com
Three Rivers	http://trfn.clpgh.org
The Times Leader (Wilkes Barre)	www.timesleader.com
Tri-StateJobs.com	www.tristatejobs.com
WesternPAHelpWanted.com	www.westernpahelpwanted.com
WilliamsportHelpWanted.com	www.williamsporthelpwanted.com

Rhode Island
The Narragansett Times (Wakefield)	www.narragansetttimes.com
Networkri.org	www.networkri.org
The Pawtucket Times	www.pawtuckettimes.com
Providence Journal Bulletin	www.projo.com
Rhode Island Department of Labor and Training	www.det.state.ri.us
Rhode Island Jobs	www.rhodeisland-jobs.com
Sakonnet Times (Portsmouth)	www.eastbayri.com
SouthernNewEnglandHelpWanted.com	www.southernnewenglandhelpwanted.com

South Carolina
Camden Chronicle Independent	www.chronicle-independent.com
Career Women	www.webcom.com/~nccareer
Carolina Career Web	www.carolinascareerweb.com
Carolina Computer Jobs	www.carolinacomputerjobs.com
Clemson University	www.clemson.edu
ColumbiaHelpWanted.com	www.columbiahelpwanted.com
Free Times (Columbia)	www.free-times.com
The Greenville News	www.greenvilleonline.com
HelpWantedCharleston.com	www.helpwantedcharleston.com
LowCountryHelpWanted.com	www.lowcountryhelpwanted.com
MyrtleBeachHelpWanted.com	www.myrtlebeachhelpwanted.com
PeeDeeHelpWanted.com	www.peedeehelpwanted.com
The Post and Courier (Charleston)	www.charleston.net
South Carolina State Jobs	www.state.sc.us/Jobs

Notes
Favorite sites, useful resources

Regional-USA (continued)

South Carolina (continued)
SumterHelpWanted.com	www.sumterhelpwanted.com
The Sun Times (Myrtle Beach)	www.myrtlebeachonline.com
UpstateHelpWanted.com	www.upstatehelpwanted.com

South Dakota
Argus Leader (Sioux Falls)	www.argusleader.com
Brookings Daily Register	www.brookingsregister.com
The Capital Journal (Pierre)	www.capjournal.com
The Freeman Courier	www.freemansd.com
Huron Plainsman	www.plainsman.com
SiouxFallsHelpWanted.com	www.siouxfallshelpwanted.com
SouthDakotaJobs.com	www.southdakotajobs.com

Southeast
MyGA.net	www.myga.net
Thinkjobs	www.thinkjobs.com

Tennessee
ChattanoogaHelpWanted.com	www.chattanoogahelpwanted.com
Chattanooga Times Free Press	www.timesfreepress.com
ClarksvilleHelpWanted.com	www.clarksvillehelpwanted.com
Daily Post-Athenian	www.dpa.xtn.net
KnoxvilleHelpWanted.com	www.knoxvillehelpwanted.com
Knoxville News Sentinel	www.knoxnews.com
Memphis Flyer	www.memphisflyer
MemphisHelpWanted.com	www.memphishelpwanted.com
Middle Tennessee-SHRM Central	www.mtshrm.org
NashvilleHelpWanted.com	www.nashvillehelpwanted.com
Nashvillejobslink.com	www.nashvillejobslink.com
Tennessee Society of CPA's Job Listings	www.tscpa.com/public/classifieds.htm
The Tennessean (Nashville)	www.onnashville.com

Texas
Advocacy, Incorporated	www.advocacy.org/jobs.html
Austin American-Statesman	www.austin360.com
AustinHelpWanted.com	www.austinhelpwanted.com
Austin Jobs	www.austin-jobs.net
Austin@Work	www.austinatwork.com
Austin Texas Jobs	www.search-beat.com/austinjobs.htm
Austin-City Jobs	www.ci.Austin.tx.us

Notes
Favorite sites, useful resources

Regional-USA (continued)

Texas (continued)

Dallas Career	www.careerdallas.com
Dallas Human Resource Management Association	www.dallashr.org
Dallas Jobs	www.dallas-jobs.net
Dallas Morning News	www.dallasnews.com
DFWHelpWanted.com	www.dfwhelpwanted.com
EastTexasHelpWanted.com	www.easttexashelpwanted.com
ElPasoHelpWanted.com	www.elpasohelpwanted.com
El Paso Times	www.elpasotimes.com
Houston Chronicle	www.chron.com
HoustonEmployment.com	www.houstonemployment.com
Houston Human Resource Management Association	www.hhrma.org/default.shtml
Houston Jobs	www.houston-jobs.net
Jobs in Higher Education Geographical Listings	http://volvo.gslis.utexas.edu/~acadres/jobs/index.html
LocalCareers.com	www.localcareers.com
LubbockHelpWanted.com	www.lubbockhelpwanted.com
Metroplex Association of Personnel Consultants	www.recruitingfirms.com
NACCB - Dallas - Ft. Worth Chapter	www.dfw-naccb.org
National Association of Hispanic Nurses Houston Chapter	www.nahnhouston.org
North Central Texas Workforce Development Board, Inc.	www.dfwjobs.com
San Antonio Express News	www.mysanantonio.com
SanAntonioHelpWanted.com	www.sanantoniohelpwanted.com
SouthTexasHelpWanted.com	www.southtexashelpwanted.com
Texas Association of Staffing	www.texasstaffing.org
Texas Healthcare & Bioscience Institute	www.thbi.org
Texas Jobs	www.txjobs.com
TexasJobs.com	www.texasjobs.com
Texas Jobs & Employment Links	www.anancyweb.com/texas_jobs.html
Texas Marketplace	www.texas-one.org
Texas Workforce Commission	www.twc.state.tx.us
TexomaHelpWanted.com	www.texomahelpwanted.com
ValleyHelpWanted.com	www.valleyhelpwanted.com
Waco, TX Jobs	www.waco-jobs.com
WichitaFallsHelpWanted.com	www.wichitafallshelpwanted.com
WT.Net	www.wt.net

WEDDLE's Helping to Maximize Your ROI ... Your Return on the Internet

Notes
Favorite sites, useful resources

Regional-USA (continued)

Utah
The Daily Herald (Provo)	www.harktheherald.com
Herald Journal (Logan)	www.hjnews.com
SaltLakeCityHelpWanted.com	www.saltlakecityhelpwanted.com
Salt Lake Tribune	www.sltrib.com
SouthernUtahHelpWanted.com	www.southernutahhelpwanted.com
Standard-Examiner (Ogden)	www.standard.net
Utah Job Store	www.utahjobstore.com
Utah Life Sciences Association	www.utahlifescience.com

Vermont
Addison County Independent (Middlebury)	www.addisonindependent.com
Burlington Free Press	www.burlingtonfreepress.com
Deerfield Valley News (West Dover)	www.dvalnews.com
NorthCountryHelpWanted.com	www.northcountryhelpwanted.com
Stowe Reporter	www.stowereporter.com
Valley News (White River Junction)	www.vnews.com

Virginia
BlueRidgeHelpWanted.com	www.blueridgehelpwanted.com
Career Pro	www.career-pro.com
The Daily Progress (Charlottesville)	www.dailyprogress.com
Danville Register Bee	www.registerbee.com
HamptonRoadsHelpWanted.com	www.hamptonroadshelpwanted.com
Human Resource Association of the National Capital Area Job Bank Listing	http://hra-nca.org/job_list.asp
The News-Advance (Lynchburg)	www.newsadvance.com
North Virginia Job Openings	www.northern-viriginia.jobopenings.net
Pilot Online	www.pilotonline.com
RichmondHelpWanted.com	www.richmondhelpwanted.com
Richmond Preferred Jobs	http://richmondpreferredjobs.com
Richmond Times-Dispatch	www.timesdispatch.com
Roanoke.com	www.roanoke.com/index.html
ShenandoahValleyHelpWanted.com	www.shenandoahhelpwanted.com
TriCitiesHelpWanted.com	www.tricitieshelpwanted.com
University of Virginia Career Planning and Placement	www.virginia.edu/~career
Virginia Biotechnology Association	www.vabio.org

Notes
Favorite sites, useful resources

Regional-USA (continued)

Virginia (continued)
Virginia-Jobs	www.virginia-jobs.com
Virginia Working 925	www.working925.com
Virginian-Pilot (Norfolk)	www.pilotonline.com
WashingtonJobs.com	www.washingtonjobs.com
Washington and Lee University	http://netlink.wlu.edu

Washington
The Columbian (Vancouver)	www.columbian.com
Communicators & Marketers Jobline (Seattle & Puget Sound)	http://cmjobline.org
Navigator Online	www.lwhra.org
The News Tribune (Tacoma)	www.tribnet.com
NorthwestWashingtronHelpWanted.com	www.northwestwashingtonhelpwanted.com
The Olympian (Olympia)	www.theolympian.com
PugetSoundHelpWanted.com	www.pugetsoundhelpwanted.com
SeattleJobs	www.seattle-jobs.com
Seattle Post-Intelligencer	www.seattlepi.nwsource.com
Seattle Times	www.seatimes.com/classified/Jobs
SoutheasternWashingtonHelpWanted.com	www.southeasternwashingtonhelpwanted.com
SpokaneHelpWanted.com	www.spokanehelpwanted.com
The Spokesman-Review (Spokane)	www.spokane.net
University of Washington	www.gspa.washington.edu
Washington Biotechnology & Biomedical Association	www.wabio.com
Washington Workforce	www.wa.gov/esd/employment.html
WesternWashingtonHelpWanted.com	www.westernwashingtonhelpwanted.com
World Careers Network	www.wcnworld.com
YakimaHelpWanted.com	www.yakimahelpwanted.com

West Virginia
Charlestown Daily Mail	www.www.dailymail.com
CharlestonHepWanted.com	www.charlestonhelpwanted.com
Clarksburg Exponent Telegram	www.cpubco.com
The Dominion Post (Morgantown)	www.dominionpost.com
HuntingtonAshlandHelpWanted.com	www.huntingtonashlandhelpwanted.com
OhioValleyHelpWanted.com	www.ohiovalleyhelpwanted.com

Notes
Favorite sites, useful resources

Regional-USA (continued)

West Virginia (continued)
Times West Virginian (Fairmont)	www.timeswv.com
Wheeling News-Register	www.news-register.com

Wisconsin
AppletonOshkoshHelpWanted.com	www.appletonoshkoshhelpwanted.com
CareerBoard.com	www.careerboard.com
ChippewaValleyHelpWanted.com	www.chippewavalleyhelpwanted.com
FetchMeAJob.com	www.fetchmeajob.com
Great Jobs WI	www.greatjobswi.com
Green Bay Press Gazette	www.greenbaypressgazette.com
HelpWantedMadison.com	www.helpwantedmadison.com
HelpWantedMilwaukee.com	www.helpwantedmilwaukee.com
The Journal Times (Racine)	www.journaltimes.com
La Crosse Tribune	www.lacrossetribune.com
LocalCareers.com	www.localcareers.com
Milwaukee Jobs	www.employmentbureau.com
Milwaukee Journal Sentinel	www.jsonline.com
University of Wisconsin-Madison School of Business Career Center	www.bus.wisc.edu/career/default1.asp
WIJobs.com	www.wijobs.com
Wisconsin Biotechnology Association	www.wisconsinbiotech.org
Wisconsin Department of Workforce Development	www.dwd.state.wi.us
Wisconsin Employment Connection	www.dwd.state.wi.us/dwe-wec/default.htm
Wisconsin.gov	www.wisconsin.gov
Wisconsin State Journal (Madison)	www.madison.com

Wyoming
Douglas Budget	www.douglas-budget.com
The Wyoming Job Bank	http://wyjobs.state.wy.us
Wyoming News.com	www.wyomingnews.com
Wyoming Tribune-Eagle	www.wyomingnews.com

Religion
Catho Online [Brazil]	www.catho.com.br
ChristiaNet	www.christianet.com
Christian Help	www.christianhelp.org
Crosswalk.com	www.crosswalk.com

Notes
Favorite sites, useful resources

Religion (continued)

Gospel Communications Network — www.gospelcom.net
Jewish Vocational Service Career Moves — www.jvsjobs.org
Ministry Connect — http://ministryconnect.org
MinistryJobs.com — www.ministryjobs.com
MinistrySearch.com — www.ministrysearch.com

Retail

AllRetailJobs.com — www.allretailjobs.com
Be The 1 — www.bethe1.com
❧ EmploymentGuide.com — www.employmentguide.com
Grocer Jobs [United Kingdom] — www.grocerjobs.co.uk
iHireRetail.com — www.ihireretail.com
In Retail [United Kingdom] — www.inretail.co.uk
Jobs Retail — www.jobsretail.com
Retail Job Net — www.retailjobs.com
Retailer News Online — www.retailernews.com
RetailResume.com — www.retailresume.com
TriStateJobMatch.com (Monster.com) — www.tristatejobmatch.com

-S-

Sales and Marketing

Access Sales Jobs — www.accessalesjobs.com
Advertising Age's Online Job Bank — http://adage.com/job_bank/index.html
Aeroindustryjobs — www.aeroindustryjobs.com
AllRetailJobs.com — www.allretailjobs.com
American Marketing Association Career Center — www.marketingpower.com/live/content.php?Item_ID=966
Autojobs.com, Inc. — www.autojobs.com
BrokerHunter.com — www.brokerhunter.com
CallCenterCareers.com — www.callcentercareers.com
CallCenterJobs.com — www.callcenterjobs.com
❧ CareerJournal.com — www.careerjournal.com
Career Marketplace.com — www.careermarketplace.com
Careers in DM-Direct Marketing — www.careersindm.com
CRN — www.crn.com/sections/careers/career.asp
DirectMarketingCareers.com — www.directmarketingcareers.com
Direct Marketing World Job Center — www.dmworld.com
Euroleaders — www.euroleaders.com
Go Partnership Limited — www.gogogo.org

Notes
Favorite sites, useful resources

Sales and Marketing (continued)

GreenBook	www.greenbook.org
iHireMarketing.com	www.ihiremarketing.com
iHireRetail.com	www.ihireretail.com
iHireSalesPeople.com	www.ihiresalespeople.com
Industry Sales Pros	www.industrysalespros.com
In Retail [United Kingdom]	www.inretail.co.uk
The Instrumentation, Systems and Automation Society Online ISA Jobs	www.isa.org/isa_es
Job.com Retail JobNet	www.job.com
Jobs4Sales.com	www.jobs4sales.com
Jobs In Marketing [United Kingdom]	www.jobs-in-marketing.co.uk
JobsNorth [United Kingdom]	www.jobsnorth.co.uk
Just Tech Sales Jobs	www.justtechsalesjobs.com
MarketingJobs.com	www.marketingjobs.com
Marketing Online	www.marketing.haynet.com
Marketing Sherpa	www.marketingsherpa.com
MediaRecruiter.com	www.mediarecruiter.com
Medical Marketing Association	www.mmanet.org
MedicalSalesJobs.com	www.medicalsalesjobs.com
Motorstaff.com	www.motorstaff.com
National Association of Sales Professionals Career Center	www.nasp.com
National Field Selling Association	www.nfsa.com
NationJob Network: Marketing and Sales Job Page	www.nationjob.com/marketing
Promotion Marketing Association Job Bank	www.pmalink.org/resources/careers.asp
NewHomeSalesJobs.com	www.newhomesalesjobs.com
1To1Jobs	www.1to1jobs.com
Pharmaceuticalrepjobs.com	www.pharmaceuticalrepjobs.com
Pro Max	www.promax.com
Retail-Recruiter	www.retail-recruiter.com
Sales Classifieds	www.salesclassifieds.com
SalesEngineer.com	www.SalesEngineer.com
Sales Giant	www.salesgiant.com
SalesJob.com	www.salesjob.com
Sales & Marketing Executives International Career Center	www.smei.org/careers/index.shtml
Sales Trax	www.salestrax.com
SellingJobs.com/BrandingJobs.com	www.sellingjobs.com
The Sixth Degree	www.thesixthdegree.com
Software & IT Sales Employment Review	www.salesrecruits.com
Tigerjobs.com, Inc.	www.tigerjobs.com
Top Sales Positions	www.topsalespositions.com
Television Bureau of Advertising	www.tvb.org/jobcenter/index.html

Notes
Favorite sites, useful resources

Science/Scientists

Academic Physician & Scientist	www.acphysci.com
AeroJobs	www.aerojobs.com
AIP Physics Career Bulletin Board	www.aip.org
Air & Waste Management Association	www.awma.org
A Job 4 Scientists	www.ajob4scientists.com
American Agricultural Economic Association Employment Service	www.aaea.org/classifieds
American Association for the Advancement of Science	www.aaas.org
American Association of Brewing Chemists	www.asbcnet.org/SERVICES/career.htm
American Association of Cereal Chemists	www.aaccnet.org/membership/careerplacement.asp
American Association of Pharmaceutical Scientists	www.aaps.pharmaceutica.com/careerCenter/job_listing.asp
American Chemical Society cen-chemjobs.org	www.cen-chemjobs.org
American Institute of Biological Sciences	www.aibs.org
American Institute of Physics Career Services	www.aps.or
American Meteorological Society Employment Announcements	www.ametsoc.org
American Psychological Society	www.psychologicalscience.org
American Society of Agronomy	www.asa-cssa-sssa.org/career
American Society of Animal Science	www.fass.org/job.asp
American Society for Cell Biology	www.ascb.org
American Society for Clinical Laboratory Science	www.ascls.org
American Society for Clinical Pathology	www.ascp.org
American Society of Clinical Pharmacology and Therapeutics	www.ascpt.org
American Society for Microbiology	www.asm.org
American Society for Gravitational and Space Biology	www.indstate.edu/asgsb/index.html
American Society of Horticultural Science HortOpportunities	www.ashs.org/careers.html
American Society of Plant Physiologists	http://baby.indstate.edu/mwaspp/index.html
American Water Works Association Career Center (Water Jobs)	www.awwa.org
Association for Applied Human Pharmacology [Germany]	www.agah-web.de
Association of Clinical Research in the Pharmaceutical Industry [United Kingdom]	www.acrpi.com
Bay Area Bioscience Center	www.bayareabioscience.org

Notes
Favorite sites, useful resources

Science/Scientists (continued)

Bermuda Biological Station for Research, Inc.	www.bbsr.edu
Biofind	www.biofind.com
BioSource Technical Service	www.biosource-tech.com
BioLinks	www.biolinks.com
BioNet Employment Opportunities	www.bio.net/hypermail/EMPLOYMENT
BioMedNet	www.biomednet.com
Bio Research Online	www.bioresearchonline.com
Bioscience Jobs	www.bioscience-jobs.com
BioSpace Career Center	www.biospace.com/b2/job_index.cfm
Bio Tech	http://biotech.mond.org/jobs/jobsearch.html
Biotechnology Calendar, Inc.	www.biotech-calendar.com
Bioview	www.bioview.com
Board of Physics and Astronomy	www.nas.edu/bpa
C & I Job Database	http://ci.mond.org
California Agricultural Technical Institute ATI-Net	www.atinet.org/jobs.asp
California Separation Science Society	www.casss.org
Cell Press Online	www.cellpress.com
Cen-ChemJobs.org	www.cen-chemjobs.org
Center for Biological Computing	http://papa.indstate.edu
Chemistry & Industry	http://chemistry.mond.org
Citysearch.com-Biotech	www.biofind.com
Controlled Release Society	www.controlledrelease.org
Earth Works	http://ourworld.compuserve.com/homepages/eworks
Easyline.co.uk [United Kingdom]	www.easyline.co.uk
Environmental Careers World	www.environmental-jobs.com
Environmental Careers Bulletin Online	www.eceajobs.com
Environmental Jobs & Careers	www.ejobs.org
Environmental Careers Organization	www.eco.org
FASEB Career Resources	http://ns2.faseb.org/careerweb
Futuro Ways	www.futureways.com
GeoWeb	www.ggrweb.com
GeoWeb Jobs	www.geowebjobs.com
GIS Jobs Clearinghouse	www.gis.umn.edu
History of Science Society	http://depts.washington.edu/hssexec
HUM-MOLGEN [Germany]	www.informatik.uni-rostock.ed/HUM-MOLGEN/anno/position.html
iHireChemists.com	www.ihirechemists.com

Notes
Favorite sites, useful resources

Science/Scientists (continued)

Institute of Physics	www.iop.org
International Society for Molecular Plant-Microbe Interactions	www.ismpinet.org/career
The Internet Pilot to Physics	http://physicsweb.org/TIPTOP
Jobs.ac.uk [United Kingdom]	www.jobs.ac.uk
Jobscience Network	www.jobscience.com
Jobscientist.com	www.jobscientist.com
LaboratoryNetwork.com	www.laboratorynetwork.com
National Organization for Professional Advancement of Black Chemists and Chemical Engineers University of Michigan Chapter	www.engin.umich.edu/soc/nobcche
National Weather Association Job Corner	www.nwas.org/jobs.html
Naturejobs	www.nature.com/naturejobs
New Scientist	www.newscientist.com
New Scientist Jobs	www.newscientistjobs.com
NukeWorker.com	www.nukeworker.com
Oceanography Society	www.tos.org
Ohio State University: College of Food, Agricultural and Environmental Sciences	http://cfaes.osu.edu/career
Optics.org	http://optics.org/home.ssi
Organic Chemistry Jobs Worldwide [Belgium]	www.organicworldwide.net/jobs/jobs.html
Physics JobLinks [Germany]	http://cip.physik.uni-wuerzburg.de/Job/job.html
Physics Today Online	www.aip.org
Plant Pathology Online APSnet	www.scisoc.org
Plasma Gate [Israel]	http://plasma-gate.weizmann.ac.il
Poly Sort	www.polysort.com
Royal Society of Chemistsry	http:chemistry.rsc.org
RPh on the Go	www.interaccess.com/ph
RPhrecruiter.com	www.rphrecruiter.com
Sci Central	www.scicentral.com
Science Careers	www.sciencecareers.org
Sciencejobs.com	www.sciencejobs.com
Science Online	www.scienceonline.org
Science Professional Network	http://recruit.sciencemag.org
Scientific American Jobs	www.sciam.com/jobs
Scijobs.org	http://scijobs.org
Space Jobs	www.spacejobs.com
SPIE Web-International Society for Optical Engineering	www.spieworks.com
Student Conservation Association	www.thesca.org

Notes
Favorite sites, useful resources

Science/Scientists (continued)

Texas A&M Poultry Science Department	http://gallus.tamu.edu/Jobs/Industry/Poultrypositions.htm
Texas Healthcare & Bioscience Institute	www.thbi.org
Utah Life Sciences Association	www.utahlifescience.com
Weed Science Society of America WeedJobs: Positions in Weed Science	www.wssa.net/weedjobs

Search Firms/Staffing Agencies/Recruiters

Accounting Position	www.taftsearch.com
AD&A Software Jobs Home Page	www.softwarejobs.com
Adecco	www.adecco.com
All Advantage	www.alladvantage.com
Alpha Systems	www.jobbs.com
American Staffing Association	www.staffingtoday.net
Amos & Associates	www.netpath.net/amos/linkstonf.htm
Aquent Partners	www.aquentpartners.com
Aron Printz & Associates	http://mindlink.net/vci/apahp.htm
The Beardsley Group	www.beardsleygroup.com
Best Internet Recruiter	www.bestrecruit.com
J. Boragine & Associates	www.jboragine.com
Buck Systems Inc.	www.bisinc.com
The Caradyne Group	www.pcsjobs.com/jobs.htm
Career Quest International	www.careerquest.com
Champion Personnel System	www.championjobs.com
Chancellor & Chancellor's	www.chancellor.com
Comforce	www.comforce.com
Corporate Staffing Center, Inc.	www.corporate-staffing.com
Cross Staffing Services	www.snelling.com/cross
Daley Consulting & Search/Daley Technical Search	www.dpsearch.com
Darwin Partners	www.seek-consulting.com
Datalake-IT.com	www.datalake-IT.com
Dawson & Dawson Consultants, Inc.	www.dawson-dawson.com
EPCglobal.com	www.epcglobal.com
ePlaced	www.eplaced.com
Erickson & Associates, Inc.	www.nursesearch.com
Executive Placement Services	www.execplacement.com
Experience on Demand	www.experienceondemand.com
Fogarty and Associates, Inc.	www.fogarty.com
Galileo Consulting	www.galileoconsulting.com/careerboard.htm
Hamilton, Jones & Koller [Australia]	www.hjk.com.au
Headhunters 4u	www.headhunters4u.com
Healthcare Recruiters	www.hcrphx.com

Notes
Favorite sites, useful resources

Search Firms/Staffing Agencies/Recruiters (continued)

The HEC Group	http://hec-group.com
Hire Quality	www.hire-quality.com
Home Page of Malachy	www.execpc.com/~maltoal
HR Connections	www.hrconnections.com
The Hunting Group's Career Network	www.hgllc.com
Hyman & Associates	www.teamhyman.com
Ian Martin Limited	www.iml.com
IMCOR	www.imcor.com
Insurance National Search, Inc.	www.insurancerecruiters.com
Insurance Overload Systems	www.insuranceoverload.com
Inter-City Personnel Associates	www.ipaservices.com
Laser Computer Recruitment [United Kingdom]	www.laserrec.co.uk
Life Work, Inc.'s Military Recruiting Group	www.lifeworkinc.com
The Little Group	www.littlegroup.com
Manpower	www.manpower.com
MarketPro	www.marketproinc.com
McGregor Boyall [United Kingdom]	www.mcgregor_boyall.co.uk
Metroplex Association of Personnel Consultants	www.recruitingfirms.com
Mindsource Software	www.mindsrc.com
National Banking Network	www.banking-financialjobs.com
1ExecutiveStreet.com	www.1executivestreet.com
On-Campus Resources, Inc.	www.on-campus.com
Pacific Coast Recruiting	www.pacificsearch.com
Pemberton & Associates	www.biddeford.com/pemberton
People Connect Staffing	www.peopleconnectstaffing.com
Premier Staffing, Inc.	www.premier-staff.com
PressTemps	www.presstemps.com
Price Jamieson	www.pricejam.com/index/le4.html
Priority Search.com	www.prioritysearch.com
Pro Match of Silicon Valley	www.promatch.org
Pro Med National Staffing	www.promedjobs.com
ProQwest, Inc.	www.proqwest.com
Provident Search Group	www.dpjobs.com
RAI	www.raijobs.com
Recruit PLC [United Kingdom]	www.newdawn.co.uk/recruit
Recruiter Networks	www.recruiternetworks.com
Recruiters for Christ	www.edmondspersonnel.com
RecruitingOptions	www.recruitingoptions.net
RGA	www.rga-joblink.com/docs/home.html
Robert Half	www.roberthalf.com
Rollins Search Group	www.rollinssearch.com
Romac International	www.romacintl.com
Sanford Rose Associates	www.sanfordrose.com
SnagAJob	www.snagajob.com

Notes
Favorite sites, useful resources

Search Firms/Staffing Agencies/Recruiters (continued)

Solomon Page Executive Search — www.spges.com
Sonasearch — www.sonasearch.com/who.htm
Stanley, Barber & Associates — www.stanleyb.com
Student Search System, Inc. — www.studentsearch.com
TechNix Inc. [Canada] — www.technix.ca
TKO International — www.tkointl.com
TMP Worldwide eResourcing — http://na.eresourcing.tmp.com/
Van Zoelen Recruitment [Netherlands] — www.vz-recruitment.nl
Volt Information Sciences — www.volt.com
Winter, Wyman & Co. — www.winterwyman.com
The Virtual Coach — www.virtual-coach.com
H. L. Yoh Company — www.hlyoh.com
Amy Zimmerman & Associates, Inc. — www.weemployyou.net

Social Service

HSCareers.com — www.hscareers.com
HSPeople.com — www.hspeople.com
iHireSocialServices.com — www.ihiresocialservices.com
National Association of Social Workers Joblink — www.socialworkers.org/joblinks/default.asp
The New Social Worker's Online Career Center — www.socialworker.com/career.htm
SocialService.com — www.socialservice.com
SocialWorkJobBank.com — www.socialworkjobbank.com
Social Work & Social Services Jobs — http://128.252.132.4/jobs
Tripod — www.tripod.com
Worklife Solutions — www.worklifesolutions.com

Statistical

American Statistical Association Statistics Career Center — www.amstat.org/careers
Bio Staticianjobs.com — www.biostaticianjobs.com
Math-Jobs.com — www.math-jobs.com
MathJobs.org — www.mathjobs.org
Phds.org — www.phds.org
StatisticsJobs.com — www.statisticsjobs.com
Statistics Jobs Announcements — www.stat.ufl.edu/vlib/jobs.html
Statistics Jobs in Austral;ia & New Zealand — www.statsci.org/jobs/

Looking for a new or better job? Looking for top talent?
Use WEDDLE's publications. See the Catalog in this book.

Notes
Favorite sites, useful resources

-T-

Telecommunications

Active Wireless	www.activewireless.com
Anywhere You Go	www.anywhereyougo.com
BroadbandCareers.com	www.broadbandcareers.com
Get the Phone	http://getthephone.com/ getthephone jobpostings.html
Hire Top Talent	www.hiretoptalent.com
New England Telecom	www.n-e-t-a.org
Porta Jobs	www.portajobs.com
RF Job Network	www.rfjn.com
Society of Satellite Professionals International Career Center	www.sspi.broadbandcareers.com /Default.asp
Telco Rock	www.telcorock.com
Telecom Careers Net	http://telecomcareers.net
Telecom Jobs	www.telecom-jobs.net
Telecom Jobsite	www.telecomjobsite.com
U GURU	www.uguru.com
UNIX admin search	www.unixadminsearch.com
Unix Review	www.unixreview.com
Telecom Engineer	www.telecomengineer.com
Telecommunication Industry Association Online	www.tiaonline.org
Telepeople	www.telepeople.com
Teletron	www.telecomcareers.com
WirelessResumes.com	www.wirelessresumes.com
Workaholics4Hire.com	www.workaholics4hire.com
Wow-Com	www.wow-com.com

Telecommuting

Mommy's Place.NET	www.mommysplace.net
Telecommuting Jobs	www.tjobs.com
VirtualAssistants.com	www.virtualassistants.com
Will Work 4 Food	www.2020tech.com/ww4f/ index.html

Trade Organizations

American Industrial Hygiene Association	www.aiha.org
Biotechnology Industry Organization	www.bio.com
Building Industry Exchange	www.building.org
Drilling Research Institute	www.drillers.com
Drug Information Association Employment Opportunities	www.diahome.org/docs/Jobs/ Jobs_index.cfm

Notes
Favorite sites, useful resources

Trade Organizations (continued)

Equipment Leasing Association	www.elaonline.com
Financial Executives Institute Career Center	www.fei.org/careers
Institute of Food Science & Technology	www.ifst.org
Institute of Real Estate Management Jobs Bulletin	www.irem.org/i06_ind_res/html/post.html
International Association of Conference Centers Online	www.iacconline.com
International Map Trade Association	www.maptrade.org
Media Communications Association International Job Hotline	www.itva.org/resources/job_hotline.htm
National Association of Colleges & Employers (NACE)	www.nacelink.com
National Association for Printing Leadership	www.napl.org
National Contract Management Association	www.ncmajobcontrolcenter.com
National Council on Compensation Insurance Careers	www.ncci.com/ncciweb/ncci.asp?If=control_panel.asp&mf=/ncci research/careers/careers.htm
National Federation of Paralegal Associations Career Center	www.paralegals.org/Center/home.html
National Field Selling Association	www.nfsa.com
National Fire Prevention Association Online Career Center	www.nfpa.org/catalog/home/CareerCenter/index.asp
National Weather Association	www.nwas.org
Petroleum Services Association of Canada Employment	www.psac.ca
Risk & Insurance Management Society Careers	www.rims.org/Template.cfm?Section=JobBank1&Template=/Jobbank/SearchJobForm.cfm
Securities Industry Association Career Resource Center	www.sia.com/career
Sheet Metal and Air Conditioning Contractor's Association	www.smacna.org
Society of Automotive Engineers Job Board	www.sae.org/careers/recrutad.htm
Society of Risk Analysis Opportunities	www.sra.org/opptys.php
Technical Association of the Pulp & Paper Industry Jobline	www.tappi.org/index.asp?ip=-1&ch=14&rc=-1
Telecommunication Industry Association Online	www.tiaonline.org

Training

American Society for Training & Development Job Bank	http://jobs.astd.org

Notes
Favorite sites, useful resources

Training (continued)

Instructional Systems Technology Jobs	http://education.indiana.edu/ist/students/jobs/joblink.html
International Society for Performance Improvement Job Bank	www.ispi.org
OD Network	www.odnetwork.org
San Francisco State University Instructional Technologies	www.itec.sfsu.edu
TCM's HR Careers	www.tcm.com/hr-careers
Training Forum	www.trainingforum.com
Trainingjob.com	www.trainingjob.com
The Training Net	www.trainingnet.com
The Training SuperSite	www.trainingsupersite.com

Transportation

AeroJobs	www.aerojobs.com
The Airline Employment Assistance Corps	www.avjobs.com
All-Trucking-Jobs.com	www.all-trucking-jobs.com
Aviation Employee Placement Service	www.aeps.com
Find a Pilot	www.findapilot.com
FindaTruckingJob.com	www.findatruckingjob.com
Global Careers	www.globalcareers.com
International Seafarers Exchange JobXchange	www.jobxchange.com
JobsinLogistics.com	www.jobsinlogistics.com
Layover.com	www.layover.com
Logistics, Materials, Handling & Supply	www.logisticsmgtcareers.com
The Mechanic	www.the-mechanic.com/jobs.html
RoadWhore.com	www.roadwhore.com
TransportationJobStore.com	www.transportationjobstore.com
TruckDriver.com	www.truckdriver.com
TruckerJobSearch.com	www.truckerjobsearch.com
Truck Net	www.truck.net
TruckingJobs	www.truckingjobs.com
TruckinJobs	www.truckinjobs.com/

-V-

Volunteer Positions

Do-It [Unied Kingdom]	www.do-it.org.uk
Volunteer Match	www.volunteermatch.org
VSO Worldwide Vacancies [United Kingdom]	http://database.vso.org.uk/jobsearch.asp

Notes
WEDDLE's Books I Want to Order

-Y-

Young Adult/Teen Positions

CoolWorks.com	www.coolworks.com
GrooveJob.com	www.groovejob.com
Part-Time Jobs	www.gotajob.com
SnagaJob.com	www.snagajob.com
StudentJobs.gov	www.studentjobs.gov
Summerjobs.com	www.summerjobs.com
Teens4Hire	www.teens4hire.org

Notes
WEDDLE's Books I Want to Order

☛ **To Place Your Order for WEDDLE's Books** ☚

Call WEDDLE's at 203.964.1888

Or use our online Catalog at www.weddles.com

WEDDLE's Helping to Maximize Your ROI ... Your Return on the Internet

WEDDLE's Catalog
Where People Matter Most

Table of Contents for Job Seekers and Career Activists — Page

- WEDDLE's 2004 Job Seeker's Guide to Employment Web Sites 310
- CliffsNotes Finding a Job on the Web 310
- WEDDLE's InfoNotes (WIN) Writing a Great Resume 311
- WEDDLE's 2004 Directory of Employment-Related Internet Sites 311
- T'is of Thee (a book about Patriotism and People) 312
- WEDDLE's WizNotes (Fast Facts on the Best Job Boards) 312

Table of Contents for Recruiters and HR Professionals

- Generalship: HR Leadership in a Time of War 313
- Extreme HR: Pushing the Envelope to World Class Performance 313
- T'is of Thee (a book about Patriotism and People) 314
- The Keys to Successful Recruiting and Staffing 314
- WEDDLE's 2004 Recruiter's Guide to Employment Web Sites 315
- Enterprise Edition of WEDDLE's 2004 Recruiter's Guide (the book on CD) 315
- WEDDLE's 2004 Directory of Employment-Related Internet Sites 316
- Enterprise Edition of WEDDLE's 2004 Directory (the book on CD) 316
- WEDDLE's Recruiter's Guide to Association Web Sites 317
- Transition Assistance for Everyone (a set of 4 books for each individual) 317
- Postcards From Space: Being the Best in Online Recruitment & HR Management 318
- Taking the High Ground in Talent Recruitment (a video seminar) 318

Would You Like to Receive Our FREE Newsletter?

WEDDLE's publishes two FREE, bi-monthly e-mail newsletters: there's one for job seekers and career activists and one for recruiters and HR professionals. Both are short publications, but filled with the latest tips and techniques for using the Internet effectively. Best of all, they're written in English, not techno-babble, so you can put the Web to work for you. To subscribe, visit the WEDDLE's Web-site at www.weddles.com and click on the sign-up link beneath the spinning globe on our Home Page or call 203.964.1888.

WEDDLE's Helping to Maximize Your ROI ... Your Return on the Internet

_____ Job Seekers and Career Activists Section _____

☛ WEDDLE's 2004 Job Seeker's Guide to Employment Web Sites

For years, job seekers have clicked and scrolled across the vast expanse of the Internet—often searching in vain for good, solid leads on serious jobs. Now, at last, they can find them!

WEDDLE's 2004 Job Seeker's Guide to Employment Web Sites is the consumer's guide to online job boards, resume banks and career portals. **Completely updated for 2004**, this handy reference carefully, thoughtfully handpicks the best of the 40,000+ employment-related sites currently available on the Internet. It supplies clear and current information about each site's services, features and fees—helping you instantly determine which sites best meet your needs. You'll find information about:

- How many and what kinds of jobs are posted in a site's job database,
- The salary ranges of the posted jobs,
- Whether the site has a resume or profile database,
- Whether the site offers interviewing assistance, employer information and job agents that will automatically notify you when a job matching your interests is posted online,
- and much, much more;

Plus you'll get FREE site updates all year long at www.weddles.com.

If you are in transition or think you might be soon, this is the book for you. Written by America's online employment expert, *WEDDLE's 2004 Job Seeker's Guide* is a cost-effective, but complete re-employment resource that will help anyone—from a first-time job seeker to a senior executive—take the Internet to their next great job!

WEDDLE's, 2004 $14.95   **ISBN 1-928734-20-0**

☛ CliffsNotes: Finding a Job on the Web

They got you through *MacBeth* and *King Lear*, now CliffsNotes can also help you discover the secrets of using the Internet to find a new or better job! WEDDLE's publisher Peter Weddle has authored this ground-breaking book for the venerable CliffsNotes series. Short, but filled with just the right information to "ace" the job market test, this book has everything you need to know about:

- Developing an effective online job search strategy
- Researching jobs and employers on the Web
- Using commercial job boards, employer sites and other job posting areas online
- Networking online
- Writing a resume for use on the Internet
- Distributing your resume over the Internet and posting it safely in resume databases
- and much more.

Whether you're a recent college graduate, a mid-career professional or a seasoned executive, this "job seeker friendly" guide will put the Internet to work for you. It is a complete online job search campaign in a booklet.

IDG/CliffsNotes, 2000 $8.99   **ISBN 0-7645-8547-9**

WEDDLE's Helping to Maximize Your ROI ... Your Return on the Internet

☞ WEDDLE's InfoNotes (WIN): Writing a Great Resume

Whether you're a seasoned professional or a first-time job seeker, a well written resume is the key to a successful job search campaign. This book helps you write a great resume without having to read some 300 page resume textbook. WEDDLE's InfoNotes (WIN): *Writing a Great Resume* is the CliffsNotes of resume guides. Written by WEDDLE's publisher Peter Weddle, it is a no-frills, step-by-step approach to:

- Selecting the best resume type for you
- Writing an effective chronological resume
- Writing an effective functional resume
- Writing an effective hybrid resume
- Designing an electronic resume for today's high tech, computerized HR Department
- Designing an Internet resume for distribution over the World Wide Web
- and much more

The perfect companion to *CliffsNotes Finding a Job on the Web*, this no-nonsense, get-the-job-done guide will show you how to write a supercharged resume that works for you. Whether you need a quick refresher or are writing your very first resume, **WEDDLE's InfoNotes** will give you everything you need to know ... and nothing more! It helps you save time and achieve career success, all in under 100 pages.

WEDDLE's, 2002 $8.99   **ISBN 1-928734-10-3**

☞ WEDDLE's 2004 Directory of Employment–Related Internet Sites

This Directory is the "address book" of employment sites on the Internet. It lists the name and the Universal Resource Locator (URL) or Internet address for over 7,500 Web-sites that operate job boards, resume databanks and career portals.

> From Monster.com, TrueCareers.com and CareerBuilder.com to HotJobs.com and CareerJournal.com ... from Cool Works, MarketingJobs.com and College Grad Job Hunter to IMDiversity, VetJobs.com and EngineerJobs.com, they're all here, right where you can find them. The Directory lists sites in the United States and in more than twenty countries around the world. It also makes it very easy for you to find exactly the sites you need because—just as in the telephone book—they are organized and listed by key categories: their occupational field, industry and/or geographic specialties.
>
> If you're looking for a new or better job anywhere in the United States or around the globe, this book can help you identify those Web-sites that will put you on the Information Superhighway to success.

Best of all, the Directory can set you apart from the "job seeker herd" online and help you find the Internet's Hidden Job Market. While everyone else is using the same old sites, you'll be able to uncover new sources of employment opportunity! So search smart online; use *WEDDLE's 2004 Directory* to find your dream job.

WEDDLE's, 2004 $49.95   **ISBN 1-928734-19-7**

WEDDLE's Helping to Maximize Your ROI ... Your Return on the Internet

☛ T'is of Thee
A Son's Search for the Meaning of American Patriotism

Peter Weddle

On September 11, 2001, the United States of America was attacked by terrorists. For those of us who lived through their horrific acts, the day began bright with hope and possibilities and ended dark with despair and fear.

> As with the attack on Pearl Harbor, however, the day's events awoke a sleeping giant. America was a nation consumed with its Pursuit of Happiness on the morning of September 11th; by the evening of that day, it was united in its determination to protect and preserve Life and Liberty for ourselves and our families, for our present and our future.
>
> This book is about American patriotism. It is an intensely personal book—not unlike *Tuesdays With Morrie*—written largely in the two years prior to the terrorist assault on this country. It was finished in the week immediately following the attack.

The book recounts the year-long "conversation" between a son and his father, between a living American and one resting in Arlington National Cemetery. Their topics range from the Vietnam War to the American Dream, but always, their conclusion is the same: America is as good, as vibrant, as hopeful as the patriotism of we, its people.

Valley Forge Press/WEDDLE's, 2001 $9.99 **ISBN 1-928734-04-9**

☛ WEDDLE's WizNotes (Fast Facts on the Best Job Boards)

Looking for a fast way to find key information about the services and features at Internet job boards and career portals? Well, look no further. Our brand, new *WEDDLE's WizNotes* has everything you need. There are separate guides for:

- ☑ Finance and Accounting Professionals
- ☑ Sales and Marketing Professionals
- ☑ Engineering Professionals
- ☑ Recent Graduates
- ☑ Executives and Managers

Each Guide describes the major sites for its audience, indicating any specialization they may have, their geographic focus, whether they have a job board or a resume database, whether they offer an automated job agent and other services for job seekers and career activists. Best of all, the Guides will fit everyone's budget!

WEDDLE's, 2004 $9.99 each

☛ To Place Your Order for WEDDLE's Books ☚
Call WEDDLE's at 203.964.1888
Or use our online Catalog at www.weddles.com

WEDDLE's Helping to Maximize Your ROI ... Your Return on the Internet

Recruiters and HR Professionals Section

☛ Generalship: HR Leadership in a Time of War   Peter Weddle
(for HR Executives, Managers & Supervisors, and those who aspire to be)

"Machiavelli's The Prince and Covey's The 7 Habits of Highly Effective People ... all rolled into one for the HR profession."   Donna Introcaso, former VP/HR iVillage and Winstar Communications

Forget about being a "strategic partner." You'll have far greater impact and earn far greater rewards being a "strategic leader" in your organization. That's the message of this provocative new book by WEDDLE's Publisher Peter Weddle.

Weddle believes that HR is in the fight of its life, a situation he calls its War for Relevancy. It is a battle for professional survival in the face of ever deeper HR budget and staff cuts and the aggressive encroachments of business process outsourcing companies. No one likes conflict, but the inescapable reality of this battle leaves HR professionals with only two choices: they can give up or they can fight back.

His prescription? HR leaders should adopt the attributes of the only executives specifically trained to lead in war: generals. This fascinating book takes you back into history to examine the battlefield exploits of the world's most successful generals. In the process, it identifies seven attributes that are the basis for successful leadership during difficult times and relates them to the challenges that confront today's HR profession.

If you're looking for practical, but outside-the-box insights on leadership, this book is for you! It is a call to arms for every HR leader and those who aspire to be. It is also the book that every CEO should read!

WEDDLE's, 2004 $19.95   **ISBN 1-928734-18-9**

☛ Extreme HR: Peter Weddle
Pushing the Envelope to World Class Performance

"Peter Weddle is a man filled with ingenious ideas." The Washington Post

You may have heard of extreme sports ... activities such as competitive surfing, mountain biking, rafting and rock climbing. They're called extreme because they involve pushing the envelope of performance and challenging assumptions about human capability and limitations. Is there a risk in such sports? Yes, of course. But the people who participate control the risk through skill and experience and, as a consequence, accomplish extraordinary feats from which they derive an extraordinary sense of accomplishment.

That notion—to venture outside the bounds of normal behavior and strive for uncommon objectives—is the theme of this book. It is a series of extreme ideas for transforming the HR Department into the thought leader, innovator, and energy source of corporate America. It offers concepts that will push you out of your comfort zone and test your willingness to do what you've never even imagined before. Unlike extreme sports, however, there is no special conditioning or athletic prowess required to practice extreme HR. All you need is the courage to think beyond the limits of what you always thought you could do as an HR professional.

From radical ideas about executive compensation and succession planning to way-way-outside-the-box approaches to decision-making for technology acquisition, this book challenges the traditional views of HR and its role in the modern enterprise.

WEDDLE's, 2004 $19.95 (expected Winter 2004)   **ISBN 1-928734-22-7**

☛ T'is of Thee
Peter Weddle
A Son's Search for the Meaning of American Patriotism

On September 11, 2001, the United States of America was attacked by terrorists. For those of us who lived through their horrific acts, the day began bright with hope and possibilities and ended dark with despair and fear.

> As with the attack on Pearl Harbor, however, the day's events awoke a sleeping giant. America was a nation consumed with its Pursuit of Happiness on the morning of September 11th; by the evening of that day, it was united in its determination to protect and preserve Life and Liberty for ourselves and our families, for our present and our future.

> This book is about American patriotism. It is an intensely personal book—not unlike *Tuesdays With Morrie*—written largely in the two years prior to the terrorist assault on this country. It was finished in the week immediately following the attack.

The book recounts the year-long "conversation" between a son and his father, between a living American and one resting in Arlington National Cemetery. Their topics range from the Vietnam War to the American Dream, but always, their conclusion is the same: America is as good, as vibrant, as hopeful as the patriotism of we, its people.

Valley Forge Press/WEDDLE's, 2001 $9.99   ISBN 1-928734-04-9

☛ The Keys to Successful Recruiting and Staffing
Barry Siegel

"If you want to get a jump start on maximizing human capital, read this book by Barry Siegel, one of the world's leading experts on staffing and recruiting."
Bruce Tulgan, author of Winning the Talent Wars

During the mid-to-late 1990s, the recruiting and staffing function moved from the back office to center stage. This paradigm shift was primarily caused by a new reality for corporate America: there were too many jobs for too few qualified people. All of a sudden, sourcing and recruiting talent became much more important to an organization's future and its overall net worth. As a result, companies invested millions of dollars to win this new War for Talent. Many valuable lessons were learned in the process.

> Then, the recession of 2001 hit, and those valuable lessons were forgotten. Many organizations abandoned their newly constructed "talent acquisition war rooms" in favor of cutting headcount to meet short term budget requirements. Despite those setbacks, however, the staffing department did not return to the back office. On the contrary, it remains in the spotlight and under a microscope.

What should recruiters and HR professionals do? You can wait for a surprise attack of new requisitions to hit you from all directions in your company; or you can wage a preemptive strike by immediately adopting the keys to successful recruiting and staffing. If you want to take charge of your future, this book is for you.

WEDDLE's, 2003 $19.95   ISBN 1-928734-17-0

WEDDLE's Helping to Maximize Your ROI ... Your Return on the Internet

☛ WEDDLE's 2004 Recruiter's Guide to Employment Web Sites

In the recruiter's arsenal of professional tools, job boards can be both the most promising—and the ones most fraught with unknowns. Which sites are candidates really visiting? Which specialize in top prospects in engineering, healthcare, sales, accounting, or IT? Which ones are worthwhile, and which a waste of time?

WEDDLE's 2004 Recruiter's Guide to Employment Web Sites answers those questions and more. This fact-filled guide plows through over 40,000 sites, winnowing out the Web's most remarkable resources for locating high caliber job candidates. Instead of the subjective opinions of so-called "pundits," it provides you with all of the information you need to make your own decisions and select the best sites for your recruiting requirements.

Completely updated for 2004, each site is described in an easy-to-read Profile, packed with <u>details</u> about:

- How long the site has been in operation
- How many people visit it each month and how long they stay there
- The occupations of its most frequent visitors
- How many candidates visit the site per job posted there
- Its job posting fees and posting period
- The number of records in its resume database
- The fee for searching the database
- Whether the site offers automatic notification of resume-job matches
- Whether the site provides status reports on postings and banner ads

Plus, you'll get FREE site updates all year long at www.weddles.com.

This is indispensable information for corporate and third party recruiters, employment managers and human resource practitioners, agency headhunters, staffing firms and consulting recruiters. <u>Volume discounts available</u>.

WEDDLE's, 2004 $27.95   **ISBN 1-928734-21-9**

☛ Enterprise Edition of WEDDLE's 2004 Recruiter's Guide to Employment Web Sites

The Enterprise Edition is *WEDDLE's 2004 Recruiter's Guide to Employment Web Sites* on a CD. It also includes a license authorizing the purchasing organization to make unlimited copies of the CD (in print or electronic format) for use within that organization.

Now, you can make WEDDLE's one-of-a-kind information about job boards and career portals available to each and every recruiter in your organization. No more passing a single copy of the Guide around the office or having to wait until someone else finishes using it. Now, every recruiter can tap the wealth of information contained in WEDDLE's Guide and put it to work for them whenever they need it. They'll be able to pick the right sites the first time and all of the time to acquire the best talent for your organization.

Best of all, the Enterprise Edition saves you money. If you bought 10 WEDDLE's Guides last year for your organization, the Enterprise Edition will save you $79.55 this year. If you bought 25 Guides last year, it will save you $498.80. Now, that's doing more with less!

WEDDLE's, 2004 $199.95

WEDDLE's Helping to Maximize Your ROI ... Your Return on the Internet

☛ WEDDLE's 2004 Directory of Employment–Related Internet Sites

This Directory is the "address book" of employment sites on the Internet. It lists the name and the Universal Resource Locator (URL) or Internet address for <u>over 7,500 Web-sites</u> that specialize in online recruiting.

> From Monster.com, TrueCareers.com and CareerBuilder.com to HotJobs. com and CareerJournal.com ... from VetJobs.com, MarketingJobs.com and College Grad Job Hunter to IMDiversity, NurseJobz.com and Engineer Jobs.com, they're all here, right where you can find them. The Directory lists sites in the United States and in twenty countries around the world. It also makes it easy for you to find exactly what you need because all of the sites are organized and listed by their <u>occupational</u> <u>field</u>, <u>industry</u> and/or <u>geographic</u> focus. If you're looking for high quality candidates anywhere in the global labor market, this book can help you find the sites they visit.

Best of all, the Directory can set you apart from the herd and increase the value you add to your recruiting assignments. While everyone else is using the same old sites, you'll be able to tap the hidden gold mines! So source smart online; use *WEDDLE's 2004 Directory* to help you find the best candidates for your openings.

WEDDLE's, 2004 $49.95   **ISBN 1-928734-19-7**

☛ Enterprise Edition of WEDDLE's 2004 Directory of Employment-Related Internet Sites

The Enterprise Edition is *WEDDLE's 2004 Directory of Employment-Related Internet Sites* on a CD. It also includes a license authorizing the purchasing enterprise to make unlimited copies of the CD (in print or electronic format) for use within that organization.

The Enterprise Edition of WEDDLE's Directory enables you to provide this powerful recruiting resource to each and every recruiter in your organization. As a consequence, they can work more efficiently and make better use of the Web's vast array of job boards and career portals.

Equally as important, you save money. If you bought 10 Directories for your recruiters last year, the Enterprise Edition will save you $99.55 this year. If you bought 25 Directories last year, you'll save a whopping $848.80! Even the CFO will be impressed.

WEDDLE's, 2004 $399.95

☛ **To Place Your Order for WEDDLE's Books** ☚
Call WEDDLE's at 203.964.1888
Or use our online Catalog at www.weddles.com

WEDDLE's Helping to Maximize Your ROI ... Your Return on the Internet

☛ WEDDLE's Recruiter's Guide to Association Web Sites
YOUR GUIDE TO THE "HIDDEN CANDIDATE MARKET"

The members of professional, technical and trade associations are some of the best candidates available in the job market. As a consequence, a growing number of associations and societies are adding job boards, resume databases and other recruiting resources to their Web-sites. The challenge for recruiters is in finding which associations offer these services and where they are located on the Internet.

WEDDLE's Recruiter's Guide to Association Web Sites solves that problem. Compiled in conjunction with the Association for Internet Recruiting (www.recruitersnetwork.com), it lists over 1,500 professional, technical and trade associations and indicates what kinds of recruiting services (i.e., job board, resume database, other) they provide. Forget the hidden job market, this book is the best guide to the "hidden candidate market" available anywhere. It's a one-of-a-kind reference for corporate and staffing firm recruiters and executive search consultants.

For example, if you're recruiting for biochemists, this guide will point you to such organizations as the American Association of Brewing Chemists, the American Association of Cereal Chemists, the American Chemical Society, the American Institute of Chemical Engineers and the Canadian Society of Biochemistry and Molecular and Cellular Biologists. While your competitors are posting jobs and searching for resumes on the same, old general purpose sites, you can be using these and similar resources to find just the qualified candidates you need.

WEDDLE's, 2002 $49.95   **ISBN 1-928734-08-1**

☛ Transition Assistance For Everyone

Traditional outplacement support is expensive and often geared to professional level or senior employees. Now, however, there is a cost-effective way for you to provide transition assistance to every employee. WEDDLE's publishes <u>a set of four books</u> designed for today's job seeker, regardless of their seniority, experience level and career field:

WEDDLE's InfoNotes (WIN): Writing a Great Resume
Called the "CliffsNotes" of resume books. In less than 100 pages, it provides everything a person needs to know to write three kinds of resumes: print (including chronological, functional and hybrid resumes), electronic (for use in today's high tech HR Departments) and Internet (for storage and transmission online).

WEDDLE's 2004 Job Seeker's Guide to Employment Web Sites
Called the "Consumer's Report" of online job boards, resume banks and career portals. This book selects 350 of the best sites, organizes them by career field, industry and geographic focus and provides a detailed description of their services, features and fees.

WEDDLE's 2004 Directory of Employment-Related Internet Sites
Called the "Yellow Pages" of the online employment industry. This book lists over 7,500 job boards, resume banks and career portals on the Internet. The sites are organized by occupational field, industry and geographic focus and listed by their name and online address.

CliffsNotes Finding a Job on the Web
This booklet is the best, single guide to using the Internet's vast array of resources for job search and career management. It introduces the most effective techniques for finding and applying to great jobs online as well as using the Internet for research, networking, resume storage and transmission, and personal development.

Together, these books retail for over $80.00 in major bookstores. In this exclusive outplacement package, WEDDLE's is offering the entire set of four books for just $59.95/set.

WEDDLE's, 20004 $59.95/set   (minimum order: 10 sets)

WEDDLE's Helping to Maximize Your ROI ... Your Return on the Internet

☞ *Postcards From Space*: Being the Best in Online Recruitment & HR Management

This unique guide provides a complete introduction to Best Practices in online recruiting. Based on WEDDLE's 6+ years of research with recruiters, job seekers and recruitment Web-sites, it presents an innovative toolkit of proven, powerful techniques for Internet-based sourcing, recruiting and Human Resource Management. Among the topics it addresses are:

- Optimizing your organization's employment brand online,
- Effective online recruiting processes, procedures and policies,
- Recruiter skills for successful online recruiting,
- Buying and installing online recruiting systems and technology,
- Designing and using recruiting metrics,
- Picking the right recruitment Web-sites for your requirements,
- Best Practices in job posting and sourcing candidate resumes,
- High impact retention strategies and tactics online, and
- Designing and operating a successful recruitment Web-site.

Unlike other books, *Postcards from Space* is written for the busy recruiter and filled with practical, easy-to-apply tips for using the Internet effectively. Each topic is covered in a number of short essays—postcards, if you will—that can be read quickly, in a single sitting. And while the concepts and strategies of using the Internet for recruiting and HR management are fully covered, the book concentrates on providing insights, tools and skills that will maximize your ROI ... your return on the Internet on-the-job.

WEDDLE's, 2003 $24.95   **ISBN 1-928734-14-6**

☞ Taking the High Ground in Talent Recruitment (Video Seminar)

The WEDDLE's Seminar has been held in cities around the country to rave reviews; in fact, more than 95% have said they found the seminars to be both very informative and very helpful.
                                                CareerJournal.com from *The Wall Street Journal*

This two-hour video presents Peter Weddle's highly popular seminar on Third Generation Internet Recruiting. Captured during a live presentation, it covers the state of the art in online recruitment, the War for Talent and the latest research on Best Practices for sourcing and recruiting top talent online. Among the specific techniques that are introduced:

- The SmartSelect™ process for picking the best sites for the best candidates
- The S-ABC-S template for writing a distinctive and compelling job posting
- The best sites for locating "A" level performers in all professions, crafts and trades
- The best online directories for finding association and key affinity group sites
- The secrets of sourcing by electronic networking
- The keys to building enduring candidate relationships online
- A communications strategy that will transform your resume database from a static stack of documents into a powerful talent reservoir
- and much, much more!

Now, you can train yourself and your colleagues on the state-of-the-art in online recruitment and never have to leave the office. Use Peter Weddle's video seminar as a refresher for seasoned recruiters and as a primer for new recruiters. There's plenty of wisdom, wit and wily ideas for everyone!

WEDDLE's, 2003 $89.00